CENTRING THE MARGINS

given a unique perspective on the work itself. Bursey's penchant for subversive literature that blazes its own path heralds a fresh voice in the world of literary criticism, one that champions in-depth analysis and erudite commentary. More than mere reviews, these are signposts for those who want to be challenged in their reading material.

Steven Mayoff, author of *Our Lady Of Steerage* and *Fatted Calf Blues*

As an essayist and book reviewer, Jeff Bursey travels the intellectual globe of fiction and comes back with original, even exotic observations. He is not a me-too commentator for experimental work, nor does he dress up the latest historical romance as literature. Instead he celebrates the genuine, the artists who don't even see the box that others try to think outside.

Maurice Mierau, author of *Detachment: An Adoption Memoir*

There may be only a handful of Canadian authors with as rigorous an approach to fiction as Jeff Bursey.

Lee D. Thompson, author of *S., a novel in [xxx] dreams*

Jeff Bursey is a highly astute literary critic. What I particularly appreciate about his reviews is the marriage of lucid thought, careful attention to detail and genuine heartfelt vision that goes into his work. Here's someone who is passionate about literature—what it can do for us and how it should be.

Victoria Best, author of *An Introduction to Twentieth Century French Literature* and co-editor of *Shiny New Books*.

Centring the Margins

Essays and Reviews

Centring
the Margins

Essays and Reviews

Jeff Bursey

*To Michael,
with thanks for the
support,
Jeff*

*2 June
2018*

zero
books

Winchester, UK
Washington, USA

First published by Zero Books, 2016
Zero Books is an imprint of John Hunt Publishing Ltd., Laurel House, Station Approach,
Alresford, Hants, SO24 9JH, UK
office1@jhpbooks.net
www.johnhuntpublishing.com
www.zero-books.net

For distributor details and how to order please visit the 'Ordering' section on our website.

ISBN: 978 1 78535 400 7
Library of Congress Control Number: 2015960678

A CIP catalogue record for this book is available from the British Library.

All contents reprinted courtesy of the following journals and publications:
*American Book Review, Books in Canada, Literary Review, Midwest Book Review, Open Letters
Monthly, The Powys Journal, The Quarterly Conversation, Rain Taxi, Requited, The Review of
Contemporary Fiction,* and *The Winnipeg Review.*

Design: Stuart Davies

Printed and bound by CPI Group (UK) Ltd, Croydon, CR0 4YY, UK

We operate a distinctive and ethical publishing philosophy in all
areas of our business, from our global network of authors to
production and worldwide distribution.

CONTENTS

Other titles by Jeff Bursey:
Verbatim: A Novel (2010)
Mirrors on which dust has fallen (2015)

Preface

1.

Water entered the basement of the two-family house we lived in when I was a child and ruined the books my elder siblings had read at my age. What remained were scattered titles with no appeal to me, yet these I repeatedly read. A few years later I took up reading Marvel Comics, *How & Why* magazines (on chemistry, astronomy, animals, and guns), and the Golden Atlas of the World six-volume series above anything else. There were never any family trips to a library, and the first two Catholic schools I attended only offered safe and unadventurous collections in each classroom. Eventually E.R. Burroughs, Tom Swift, and the Hardy Boys came along. Seeing my father read a particular book introduced me to paperback reprints of pulp novels—The Shadow, The Spider, The Avenger, Doc Savage, and G-8 and His Battle Aces—which led to devouring real-life histories of the Mafia alongside the science-fiction collection of my eldest brother. Reading, then, was first based on numbing repetition—how many times would Tarzan order an ape or a lion to do his bidding or come across isolated Romans?—and then on brutality and crime, speculative and fantastic tales, and in my early teens books by and about the Marx Brothers.

Books considered "children's classics" played no part, then, in my formative reading. When finally introduced to Hans Christian Andersen at age 21, by a well-meaning woman whose aim was to distract me while I waited in Emergency after tearing a tendon falling down stairs, how lucky I felt about my childhood reading, that it had contained photographs and charts about animals and railway tracks, and maps of defunct countries, rather than the stories in the collection she had with her. *Gulliver's Travels*? Encountered first at Memorial University of Newfoundland under the hapless direction of a Jesuit teacher named Nash; a man, the women in the night class often said (teachers by day who were doing courses for an M. Ed.), who knew everything—why, "just one look at his office and all those books and you know you can't tell him nothing he don't already know." (Yes, they were teachers and they spoke like that.) Since some of these women were married and showed each other pictures of their offspring, I hoped there were things he didn't know. So another classic safely sequestered from me, this time behind the rotting drapery of an education some 50 years old.

MUN's English department curriculum reflected staid, English, or with-it taste that would never really upset anyone or anything: Spencer, Blake, Samuel Johnson, *Tess of the d'Urbervilles* (a core text in three courses), Donne, Dickens, and Shakespeare, and Barthes and Derrida. The Canadian fare veered from gritty realism written in the early decades of the 21st century to mid-century pastoral nonsense that pretended Modernism didn't exist. Neither spoke to hormonal, active eighteen- and nineteen-year-olds. These classics constituted English literature, and this was what we would read and study the rest of our lives?

The classrooms of three exceptional professors (Leona Doerksen, Alan Hall, and Bernice Schrank) were home to more vibrant works—Dos Passos, Faulkner, Joyce, Robertson Davies (who had an attraction for a time), and plays by many European and United Statesian writers that were unpredictable. They were fine, especially Ibsen, *The Big Money*, and *Absalom, Absalom!*, but they were only ever fine enough. Nothing explosive. Then I found Henry Miller's *Tropic of Cancer* and *Tropic of Capricorn* at a used bookstore. That might be 1980. Nothing (in writing) matched the experience of reading those two books, and my concept of literature changed forever.

2.

In 1986 Terry Eagleton gave what was called the Pratt lecture at

MUN. Dressed in a loose-fitting, or possibly sagging, cardigan seemingly made from oatmeal or at least that colour, Eagleton spoke at length, in dry tones, no affectation of style or vocal modulation permitted, on "The End of English." It's too long ago to recall much except for an invocation of Conrad, and other writers at the margins who had, or so I recall, moved into the homes of English literature and, specifically, writing in Britain. If that's not quite accurate, it's what I imagine he said.

My choice to write an MA thesis on Miller's work provoked the disapproval of various faculty members (with Bernice Schrank defending me and my work at each step), and placed me on the margins of the English department. Research led to Lawrence Durrell, the Powys family, Wyndham Lewis, Louis-Ferdinand Céline, Anaïs Nin, and from there to the Surrealists, Raymond Queneau, Blaise Cendrars, and so on. I never looked back at what one had to read to be considered this or that kind of well-read reader or, increasingly, informed author as I started to write plays and, in time, fiction. A respect for honest criticism and consideration of unordinary works coupled with an appreciation for the byways, shady avenues, and open boardwalks of fiction, building on my disorganized early reading, meant that I gravitated to obscure works, and that they became the most important for me relatively early on.

3.

All that is to help explain the contents of this book. The figures discussed here are, for the most part, often put out by smaller presses, and can be hard to find, offbeat, or new, as many have only recently been translated into English. Since roughly 2001 I've reviewed Céline and Harry Mulisch, Aleksandr Solzhenitsyn and Chandler Brossard, Anne Finger and Karl Ove Knausgaard, Magdalena Tulli and Lance Olsen. Assigned books often included authors who were absolute ciphers to me; others I chose out of curiosity or familiarity. Those looking for a deeper connection, a thematic or psychological underpinning, are welcome to do so.

There is no theoretical apparatus underlying the approach taken herein, as each book, to my way of thinking, requires its own approach, if you want to view them as artworks and not treat them as exemplars of this or that critical discourse. (In *Infinite Fictions*, David Winters reviews books by Eagleton and D.N. Rodowick that show how theory, in any case, is in a parlous state.) In the pages that follow there are no trendy, pithy, or apposite quotations from Benjamin, Lacan, Deleuze, or Cixous. After giving a reading from my first book, *Verbatim: A Novel*, at a German university in 2013 the floor opened up to questions, and a mature student from the US asked me if, while writing the novel, I had done so with literary theories in mind. He looked so eager for a positive answer and I didn't feel like disappointing him in front of 50 of his peers by saying no. My made-up answer — "subaltern writing" — satisfied and kept an argument from breaking out.

I should return to a subject that has been partly answered, and, though it takes many forms, is really just one basic question: "Why *that* writer and not this better-known and more influential one?" Once I strayed from the university's curriculum requirements I kept wandering. The writers I chanced upon or who I was led to, viewed in one way, perhaps took up time that others might have occupied, others who possibly might have pleased me as much. Who can say? There's no universal hierarchy (camouflaged as a top 50 or 100 books you should read) presented in this collection. Yet would I trade reading Mati Unt for reading John Updike? There is much written on the second figure's books and little (in English) on the first, whose writing I appreciate much more for its cleverness of approach and ideas, a lively style, intelligence, warmth, humanity, and inventiveness. Canadian poet and critic Carmine Starnino has this description, reprinted in

Lazy Bastardism: Essays & Reviews on Contemporary Fiction, of the two editors of a poetry anthology that featured obscure poets: "they belong to a generation that has sided with the neglected, maligned and unfairly out-of-print."[1] Any reviewer I admire takes on the role of an advocate at some point. Some figures require defending, some deserve to be brought to the attention of others, and there is an erratic compulsion to educate the public, as well as to counter the forests of press devoted to the Dan Browns and Alice Munros who are always with us.

There are many ways to teach writing; I know of only one that worked for me, and that is to read writers who, it turns out, do things that delight. All the writers in this collection, for the most part, have taught me something, even if in the negative.

4.

From the contents page, and from these few words, it's obvious that what W. Vollmann, W. Lewis, or J.C. Powys think in the political sense matters much less than how they write. My own novels try not to side with this or that set of ink spots that are called characters but to present ideas and systems in which they reside. I've also worked for 23 years in a non-partisan environment. Yet when provoked I can be drawn into speaking out polemically in defense of so-called unusual writing, such as when, in 2011, an award-winning Canadian writer, Rabindranath Maharaj, originally from Trinidad, made eye-catching statements that appeared on 28 September in *Quill & Quire*'s Quillblog, in an article titled "Writers' Trust shortlist trumpets unsung Canadian talent." His words fit into debates current at that time in England (concerning the Booker) and in the US (around the National Book Awards), and that seem to be going on still.

In his role as a juror for the Writers' Trust awards, Maharaj reflected on the just-released shortlist with Stuart Woods, who quoted him as saying:

> I believe what these writers have done and what they're doing
> is they're very quietly innovative without drawing attention
> to their innovation. And they're innovative in the sense that
> their books are more accessible – it's more reader-friendly in
> many ways... The elements of good storytelling are still
> there.[2]

At the best of times (whenever they were), innovative writers—
often called experimental, though a more accurate term might be
exploratory—have had a hard time getting published. They
create the sorts of things *Writers' Digest* ignores, and which annoy
mainstream critics and book reviewers. Their style and manner of
presentation draws attention. They are all relatively under-read,
but their so-called difficult fictions—what people in their corner
term artful and challenging works—after some time become
more comprehensible. What about those operating in the same
way now who don't have history (and judges) on their side? It's
important to emphasize that such writers, due to their small
number, limited press runs, and tiny amount of publicity, have
never posed a threat to the mainstream. It's easy to find books by
authors like Stephen King, Jonathan Franzen, J.K Rowling, or
Jodi Picoult (due to the mass number of their sales and the effect
on the marketplace, writers of what can be called *conglomerature*);
it's harder to find books by Harry Mathews, Alexandra Chasin,
and A.D. Jameson. Where Margaret Atwood and other brand
names are granted much leeway in sentiment and space in the
press no matter if what comes out is average or bad, novels that
don't adhere to some perceived notion of normal writing are
received in a less friendly way. They are sometimes considered
not art but an affront.

Maharaj's preference for reader-friendly books can be interpreted as a chiding dismissal of those who aim to write

something unusual. He is saying that innovative (Canadian) writers who are too upfront and pushy about their work should dial it down, on the way to knocking it off entirely. That's not so very far from Dale Peck's dismissal of, among many others, Rick Moody.

That sort of blinkered, divisive view of writing has been addressed many times. One of the best examinations of it comes from Gabriel Josipovici, to my mind a brilliant novelist, in his essay "Conclusion: From the Other Side of the Fence, or True Confessions of an Experimentalist." It begins: "It is a shock to any artist who has only thought of getting things 'right,' of pinning down that elusive feeling which is the source and end of all creative activity, to wake up one morning and find himself labelled 'experimental.'"[3] He further writes that reviews of two of his books

> seemed to share the same assumptions: there are writers and there are experimental writers; the 'experimental' is a sub-branch of fiction, rather like teenage romances or science fiction perhaps, but differing from them in being specifically highbrow, and, like other highbrow activities, such as abstract painting and classical music, it is totally unconnected with the real world; however, we should tolerate this for the health of art (and to show how tolerant we are).

Since the date of that collection we have moved further backwards: lower readership, straitened times, and the arts under attack from many directions and forces. Maharaj's remarks could be regarded as dumb, idle chit-chat were he not respected for his novels and short stories, and also a teacher who has the opportunity to shape and influence future writers. When such a figure starts dictating what's reader-friendly and casts aside what's writerly, then literary fiction has an additional problem.

Novelists, playwrights, short-story writers, and poets of

every kind are unified in at least one essential way: within the communicative act that is the piece of fiction or the villanelle resides what we want to say and how we want to say it. It's mostly *how* things are said that creates barriers. There is a belief out there in some quarters that experimental/exploratory fiction is made "difficult" by authors out of orneriness or to show how smart they are, and that what's present in the works of, for example, McElroy could have been conveyed in a more reader-friendly way, as if the style and structure got in the way of the only important thing: the story. (William Gass has a good response to that: "Story is what can be taken out of the fiction and made into a movie. Story is what you tell people when they embarrass you by asking what your novel is about."[4]) Maharaj tries to assure any potential readers of fiction that the books on the shortlist don't deny them that old, preserved cherry: "The elements of good storytelling are still there." Because everyone knows that innovative writers like John Barth can't be trusted to tell a story well, and they certainly don't do it straight. "Even this crew," he seems to be saying, "barely innovative as they are—innovative-lite!—can still keep you seated around the campfire. Trust me." The ebook and big block stores aren't going to kill printed literary fiction alone. "And they're innovative in the sense that their books are more accessible…" If Maharaj is saying what I think he is, then the only innovation he can stand to see is that which makes books accessible, not the kind that makes them artworks that upset complacency and that live down through the centuries.

I see in Maharaj's remarks an unspoken preference for conservative ways of expressing thoughts that, if fostered, will lead in time to a reduced imagination producing, in the main, conservative thoughts. At that point innovation will be unwelcome, and innovative creators, already looked at askance, will be scorned (just as Josipovici is scorned in England by the juries of the Booker and other awards). This is not the kind of community of writers anyone would reasonably choose to be associated with. Curtis White put it nicely: "Each new work of fiction or poetry is the presentation of a world within which we might choose to live."[5] What worlds do critics invent? Stepping away from the regular formulas alarms those who think that this act means a writer is not being realistic (as if we all could agree on what's real). If writers are encouraged to create versions of the world in whatever fashion they choose—and some versions may take work to decipher—then there can only be anarchy, in their minds. To write against the order—against corporatism, bland politeness, and muted approaches—is now to be reader-unfriendly.

But if one's writing is true to what one thinks and feels, and results in work that is new, and shows independence of thought and skill, is this a shameful deed? Should writers who do that be classed as showy, impolite, and not worthy of recognition? The type of achievement that I'm talking about does demand of a reader that he or she work to get the most out of a novel or poem or whatever it might be.

We live (have always lived) in stressful times. People will respond as they choose, and so there is going to be indignation, rudeness, and other unseemly-seeming feelings in any country's literary fiction. Those are legitimate feelings, and they have their place on a spectrum of responses to the world around us. For those who want good manners there's no shortage of books to choose from. I don't deny the mainstream authors their audience. However, others will seek to create new work in new forms, and if they're viewed as rude threats, that's not a bad thing. These reviews were often written with the explorers and the unruly in mind.

5.

That flood destroyed a quantity of books, some of which may

have been good, but that'll never be known. I do know that reading over and over the motley lot left high and dry meant that when new books entered my compass I grabbed them. That hunger hasn't left me, and perhaps accompanies my choice of what to review. Legions will tackle the latest book by X and leave Lance Olsen alone. Chris Eaton deserves a wider audience, and I'm waiting for his next novel, but it's most likely that its appearance will be somewhat muffled or completely obscured by the demand for coverage in the shrinking number of book-review pages of titles that supposedly matter more.

Today's readers and writers hunt through blogs (which can sometimes offer up gems, but also contain misspelt summaries of plots) to do what readers and writers throughout history commonly have done: gather together those works (often conflated with *those authors*) who feed our creative soul and are some kind of kin. Why not speak out for this intentional community? We need more pamphleteers for writers we believe in who are not seen much by the general audience to bring them into visibility, not because these authors need us (though they might) but because we need these authors who explore new terrain with equipment of their own devising. I've worked on bringing less popular works into the centre of the conversation. Critic Warren Motte suggests that we "...can take the notion that we inhabit the margins of things and turn it to our advantage. Far from something that limits us, we can reconfigure that notion as something that frees us and expands our horizon of possibility."[6] Maybe this collection will be seen as some kind of aesthetic-political act, as a quixotic crusade—possibly as elitism. Depending on who's reading, it can be any number of things. So can the books that follow. I hope in this collection to have adjusted, if only for a time, their position, as these authors and their works deserve to be rescued from the outer limits of criticism and brought to the centre of life.

*

Abbreviations have been used for journals (not *Requited*):
ABR *American Book Review*
BC *Books in Canada*
EBR *Electronic Book Review*
LR *The Literary Review* (US)
MBR *Midwest Book Review*
OLM *Open Letters Monthly*
PJ *The Powys Journal*
QC *The Quarterly Conversation*
RT *Rain Taxi*
RCF *The Review of Contemporary Fiction*
TWR *The Winnipeg Review*

Jeff Bursey
Charlottetown, Winter 2016

Part I: Panorama

[SIC], by Davis Schneiderman
QC, 14 March 2014

Davis Schneiderman is a prolific author of conceptual works of fiction, as well as criticism on William Burroughs and surrealism. *[SIC]* is volume two of his *DEAD/BOOKS* trilogy, and to help locate his newest fiction work a few words must be said about volume one, *Blank* (2011), also published by Jaded Ibis Press.

I started reading *Blank* in August of last year in Ottawa's airport, which turned out to be propitious, alternately thumbing its pages and staring at the wares of the duty-free store. Turning in another direction I could see runways and observe how the sun and sky were very bright. All this while I waited to board my flight to British Columbia, regretting that Air Canada, our excuse for a national airline, had decided the plane should stop in Toronto. Direct flights are preferable. *Blank* is a direct flight. It takes place in the air, has a small cast of characters (two of whom fall in love, then out), and its activity occurs in a limited span of time.

Usually on planes you have a seatmate who is forgotten soon after you've touched down. But in this novel people insist on knowing each other, and they grow affectionate, and then there occurs a disagreement that sunders everything. I had reached that part by the time my row was called to board. Yet the book had pages to go, and I could hardly wait to see what happened. Normally I don't take page-turners on a trip. Heck, I barely even read books with quotation marks around the speech anymore. But that's a digression, and, as implied, *Blank* is anything but.

Most books that take place on airplanes focus on characters, frightened ones, supercilious ones stretching their limbs in Business Class and explaining to the man next to them (it's always a man) how their sales trip went, children, the sleepers who snore undeterred by the yaw and pitch of the journey, and those nervous about being right next to the emergency exits. In the chapter "They argue," a terrible and sudden hole in the lead couple's tender and growing spiritual bond is shown, as if a part of the plane's body had been ripped away, and they are exposed to the pitiless cold. Depressurizing occurs, visibly to them, and, if we have allowed ourselves to be engaged, to us as well. The next chapters, "More obstacles" and "They fall apart," further illustrate the decline. Yet, in this case, what we normally get is not present. We don't hear the characters open their saddened hearts, or close them up, or anything. It's not the usual set of noises heard on planes that drowns out their words. What Schneiderman has done, and how it continues in [SIC], is more evocative.

But first let me continue talking about *Blank*. We associate noise with pandemonium, waterfalls, industrial sites, revolutions, and airplane travel—from the beeps of machinery to the incessant roaring of engines. We have made a special category of white noise. It's *that* category Schneiderman has given a twist, for, other than the titles to the 20 chapters given in the table of contents, and the author's name and the title of the book at the top of all the pages, in *Blank* there are no words. Instead there are ragged images of the sky (or many skies), one or maybe two per chapter, and each chapter is 10 pages long. Everything I've imagined that could happen in a chapter called "They encounter an animal" might not be very original, but it springs from and into the space supplied to my mind. Another person reading the same chapter would fill it with different material. Nevertheless, *Schneiderman's* name and *his* title top the pages and own the book, the setting, figures, and timeframe (this book adheres to the Aristotelian unities), as well as the impetus for us to re-think the contents.

Blank, the first volume of *DEAD/BOOKS*, is a bound collection of paper not much at variance from a blank journal empty of thought but full of potential. One can write anything in it, as I wrote a rough draft of the first few paragraphs of this review on that plane trip, but I can see how other readers might view *Blank* as a con, or a work of cleverness that might at best be witty but, more likely, does not possess value. It could be seen as an unpromising academic exercise.

I didn't make it up that I regarded it as a page-turner, for intellectual audacity can be as stimulating as any plot featuring dames, money, and guns. *Blank*, in my view (though this may be a wish in excess of what Schneiderman's aiming to achieve), takes minimalism as far as it can go in the hopes that writers will give up on it for-fucking-ever. Yet even with everything removed, save for tiny exceptions, the ghostly trace of the author remains, something addressed by the antepenultimate and penultimate chapters: "You die" and "I die." Yet we don't have the death (or dearth) of the narrator or the author since there's one more chapter and the headers, the word "novel" on the cover, and so on. Plus, I refute the aim of the book, to whittle down what needs to be shown and said (and am encouraged or teased into doing that), by scribbling on those white sheets what can loosely be called my own thoughts.

In 2011 Andrew Gallix, in the *Guardian*, wrote a piece on unread difficult books, and he mentioned "an anthology of blank books [edited by Michael Gibbs] entitled *All Or Nothing*." We can consider *Blank* as continuing that line. Kenneth Goldsmith's prefatory essay "Why Conceptual Writing? Why Now?" in *Against Expression: An Anthology of Conceptual Writing* (2011) contains these useful lines: "What has happened in the past fifteen years has forced writers to conceive of language in ways unthinkable just a short time ago. With an unprecedented onslaught of the sheer quantity of language… the writer faces the challenge of exactly how best to respond." In volume one of his trilogy, Schneiderman edged near to muteness, but in *[SIC]* he has positioned himself, the work, and us in a new spot. His latest book is filled with words. None of them are his.

Oulipian Daniel Levin Becker, in his introduction written in 99 notes (riffing on the late Raymond Queneau's *Exercises in Style*, where one anecdote is written in 99 ways), states at the outset: "It is not without mixed feelings that I realize I have agreed to write the only original words, so to speak, in this book." Note 12 comments on the exactitude of note 1: "But then of course what is an original word?"

[SIC] proper starts with the table of contents, broken into three sections: "Part 1: From (Pre-1923)"; "Part 2: The Borges Transformations (1939–present)"; "Part 3: @ (Post-1923)". These pages tell us that everything to come is written by someone other than Schneiderman. To choose a few examples, after a definition of the word "from," part 1 opens with Caedmon's Hymn (7th-and 8th-century), and moves forward in time through *Utopia*, the journals of Captain Cook, a poem by Keats, *The Confidence-Man*, and ends with *Ulysses*. All of these are pre-copyright, while the other parts contain works that rest in the public domain, and Schneiderman has signed his name to each and every item. "Why are so many writers now exploring strategies of copying and appropriation?" Goldsmith asks in the same essay quoted above. "It's simple: the computer encourages us to mimic its workings. If cutting and pasting were integral to the writing process, we would be mad to imagine that writers wouldn't explore and exploit those functions in ways that their creators didn't intend." Further: "When I dump a clipboard's worth of language from somewhere else into my work and massage its formatting and font to look exactly like it's always been there, then, suddenly, it feels like it's mine."

In part 2 Schneiderman does just that by taking "Pierre Menard, Author of the Quixote," by Borges, and running its original Spanish through several language-translation programs, veering from Italian to Estonian, to Japanese, and ending in

English. The result is what he did more than what he created, and the product is mostly gibberish that is unlike any text we know, let alone the original (for original, read: the one we may be familiar with), but it does bear certain marks found in what Borges wrote. Part 3 is filled with documents from after 1923, the year of advances (or retardations, depending on the point-of-view) in copyright law, such as chain letters, songs, and recipes that can lead into speeches, a computer virus, and a series of tweets.

Schneiderman says to Levin Becker in the introduction: "'You don't really need to '"read"' it, as it is a work of conceptual literature.'" That's mischievous, a joke on the enterprise, on a reader's abilities, and on the way the book can be approached. (Or perhaps what's also meant is that we can just follow the spectral figure in the black-and-white photographs by Andi Olsen, a white humanoid that has a lot of time to itself, in Paris and other places, and leave the text alone.) Yes, it's more an idea about what to do in literary fiction than something by Jonathan Franzen, but it is an exciting leap, and, from my perspective, it is also an anthology of prose and pros (Chaucer, Shakespeare, Melville, and computer programmers among them), a radical re-visioning of the familiar *Norton Reader*.

The purpose of *[SIC]* is manifold: to unsettle expectations, to show what we can do to and in the novel, to make us revisit the concept of originality and copying, to transform before our eyes other people's words and conceits into new shapes and designs that, as Goldsmith said, make them "mine." Schneiderman appears to be without illusions as to the uniqueness of this or any work, and the third volume, *INK*, will carry the project forward into new terrain. As for *[SIC]*, you may think: Why buy this book when I have the originals already? Not in these versions you don't. Try though Davis Schneiderman does to remove himself, something singular about his mind resides in this work of fiction despite and amongst the borrowing, and we can't help but notice it.

*

The Sea-God's Herb: Essays & Criticism, 1975–2014, by John Domini
TWR, 22 December 2014

In Canada, we lack published collections of essays, reviews, and articles by garlanded fiction writers like Wayne Johnston or Anne-Marie MacDonald on the work of their peers and the state of writing generally. The occasional critical remarks are often confined to media interviews, enthusiastic outpourings on the backs of books, and blogs. There is no one explanation for this awkward silence in the national conversation; rather, there are as many as there are prospective writers. When writers don't assess at length what they and their colleagues do, then there is a loss of sustained and, hopefully, intelligent commentary on the abilities of their fellow practitioners, and the startling self-revelations that can come from a sincere engagement with others' works.

Partly for those reasons I was drawn to John Domini's newest book, and additional reasons can be summed up quickly: his reviews in *American Book Review*, which are admirable for their concision and insightful, idiosyncratic analysis; his introduction of writers unknown before (to me); and the fact that the table of contents of *The Sea-God's Herb* reveals interests that overlap partially with mine when it comes to postmodern US fiction. In addition, there are reviews of select figures from other countries. The canvas is broad. Someone might ask: Does this selection of reviews cohere? Do they tell us something about the books and about Domini, too?

Aware of such questions, he addresses them in the opening essay, "The Sea-God's Herb: News About Narrative, 1975–2014." After bringing in examples of previous fiction writers who were also critics, Domini indicates that he wants to "honor my elders," and that it's "the idea of 'help,' you see, that drives the critic and essayist in me… It keeps yanking me to the desk: a brief on behalf of the most modern and post-modern. Such work has been so badly misunderstood that I feel I can be useful." What he calls *help* may be termed the desire to incite others to read books that would otherwise be missed or ignored, when not damned by a Dale Peck for their distinction from most fare.

At the risk of putting a word in Domini's mouth, I suggest that some literary critics surprise themselves by assuming the role of pamphleteer for a movement or a subset of authors. There are dangers for creative writers (Domini is a poet and novelist) in being an advocate as they "often grumble about how higher impulses get diffused when they have to generate the low-level noise of a book review," and there is, too, the fact that "any honest writer has to recognize how his or her arguments can become glib, a kind of shrink-wrap that risks suffocating the artwork under consideration." Yet Domini persists, and his book "as a whole amounts to a defense of artists taking chances." This is, simultaneously, also a celebration of those who take risks in imagining and publishing books that are not in the mainstream. Domini does this without pretension and without submitting his likes and dislikes to a critical ideology.

"Against the 'Impossible to Explain:' The Postmodern Novel & Society," the second essay in the collection, expresses his motivations clearly: "Here's the problem. You decide to try some reading outside the ordinary, a novel that doesn't have the usual earmarks, and it proves interesting, satisfying, but you don't entirely understand why, and when you look for help, an illuminating review or something, you can't find any." What this indicates is that in "the millennial US, for those who venture an unconventional approach to book-length fiction, criticism just hasn't been doing its job." The impulse rises to contribute, in however small a way, in whatever discussion is going on about a book or writer, but it's not always easy to be heard when one must fight an inculcated resistance to postmodernism present in "the major review outlets [where] the write-up will be vicious." Domini moves from Carole Maso and William Gass to Richard Powers, Michael Martone and Steve Erickson as he relates how their worth has been overlooked in their homeland. This essay exposes the fondness, laziness and cowardice (my words) exhibited by many critics as they choose to review the same books by the same people every year while ignoring new names and small presses. (That same mentality is behind the surprise, often disguising a mixture of annoyance and incomprehension, one hears when X or Y doesn't appear on award long- or short-lists.) The sharpness of tone is appreciated.

Domini divides the nearly 40 reviews into seven sections: "Early Tide," "Second Tide," "Distant Moons," "Fresh Tide," "Other Gravities," "Coming Tide," and "Galactic Pole." A belief that leaps out of an early review—a consideration, from 1979, of Guy Davenport's short-story collection *Da Vinci's Bicycle*—is that fiction can have "an impact in the nervous system as well as the centers of cognition," and one sees this conjoined response endure through to the latest review, a sign that Domini has neither become wrapped up in his own work and unable to recognize the importance of what others create, nor is he jaundiced or depressed when reading the works of others (unlike, for example, novelist Tim Parks, resident English sourpuss of the *New York Review of Books*, who seems despairing of literature). Both new methods of presentation and old favourites appeal to him.

Scattered among the shorter pieces are longer appreciations. Donald Barthelme is the subject of "The Modernist Uprising," and this is preceded by an equally long and even finer appreciation of John Barth's novel *LETTERS* (both were teachers of Domini; their works, like those of Italo Calvino and Dante, are touchstones in this collection), the second allowing the chance for comparison of a postmodernist master with Vladimir

Nabokov and Thomas Mann. Works by John Hawkes and Robert Coover are considered in tandem, resulting in this conclusion: "If these two books wear their ideas on their sleeves more than a popular novel would, it's because they don't want the smug voyeuristic distance a popular novelist maintains, rather pursuing the wholehearted commitment of senses and mind a real artist must have." That sentence illustrates discrimination with a swinging rhythm. Domini can be blunt about writers one would guess he'd approve of; he advises readers to pick up Thomas Pynchon's disappointing *Vineland* nevertheless "for the occasional winning passages and conflagrations, the few grapes that aren't sour."

After considering progenitors of postmodernism Domini looks at the next generation, in this case, among others, Toni Morrison, Russell Banks, Gilbert Sorrentino, and Stephen Dixon. When considering foreign writers in "Distant Moons," among the unsurprising names for someone with his tastes (Calvino, W.G. Sebald) is Michael Ondaatje's *The English Patient*. We disagree on the value of Alain Mabanckou's *African Psycho*, but he has me intrigued by Paul Ableman, whose novel *I Hear Voices* "stands as another example of the wild freedoms embraced by European fiction since 1945, freedoms still only fitfully understood on this side of the Atlantic."

In the section "Fresh Tide" Jay Cantor receives compliments for his novel *The Death of Che Guevara*, and how he "has so thoroughly assimilated the Latin American ambiance that he's taken on its music: hyperbolic and exclamatory, free with metaphor and repetition, always ready to snap off an epigram..." Like Morrison and Maso, Jaimy Gordon is regarded highly in an essay from 2012, while Lance Olsen's *Head in Flames* brings out this reaction: "I've rarely experienced so deep a chill in reading that sets such a formal challenge." This remark alerts a reader to an exciting voice and underlines how emotion and impetus to thought continue to fuel Domini's critical fire.

The third-last category, "Other Gravities," deals with an Italian comic book, an art installation at the Guggenheim of Italian designs, *The Sopranos*, and the work of poet and essayist W.S. Di Piero.

Concentrating on recent works by mostly younger novelists, the next section, "Coming Tide," opens with an intriguing review of Brian Evenson's *Open Curtain* that contains advice on the novelist's desire to be "respectful." *"Respectful*: the word worries me. A talent like this should take on realism with the same savagery as he's attacked other modes." Asking an author to write differently than he or she does is fraught with condescension or insensitivity, but I think what Domini is getting at is that he senses capacities in Evenson that deserve encouragement. Zachery Mason is presented as a successor to Calvino with his novel *Lost Books*, and the works of that Italian Oulipian (among other things) re-appear, as a negative image, in the next essay on Sorrentino's terrific last novels, which receive praise for "their reassertion of emotional content, even in constructs that have no truck with convention."

Dawn Raffel's *Further Adventures in the Restless Universe* contains some short stories that are "nothing short of masterful." Catholic in taste, Domini can admire a work of such brevity while also believing that Roy Kesey's *Pacazo*, a 500-plus-page take on *Don Quixote*, "generates a fresh and powerful reminder of what fiction can accomplish at full length." Reviews of books by Blake Butler (*Ever*) and Matt Bell (*The Collectors*) once more bring out the enthusiast in Domini, as when he says that these "very-small-press books afforded me some of my most cleaning and enjoyable reading, recently—a terrific experience..."

The final category, "Galactic Pole," comprises one essay from 2009, "Tower, Tree, Candle: Dante's *Divine Comedy* & the Triumph of the Fragile." New translations of Dante's central work have come out recently (see Robert Pogue Harrison, "Dante: The Most Vivid Version," *New York Review of Books*, 24

October 2013), as well as critical books on it (such as *Reading Dante: From Here to Eternity*, by Prue Shaw). There may be the understandable motive on Domini's part to join in speaking about a poet whose work appeals to him deeply. A canto from "Paradiso" provides the title of this collection, and Dante is invoked throughout. Over several pages Domini examines how Peter Jackson's version of *The Lord of the Rings* reveals "the *Comedy*'s contemporary penetration into image and meaning," and he gives sufficient evidence to make this notion worth considering.

By the end of *The Sea-God's Herb* we have encountered an abundance of new novels, short stories, and poetry from the US, and seen certain features that recur: Domini is attracted to the mythic, the intellectually alive, and, to use a word from his last essay, the "freefall" effect caused in readers by fiction that refuses to provide final answers. Pithy judgments and one-liners, negative appraisals and genuine endorsements, are presented with verve and personality. However, as Daniel Green asked in his review of the book posted at Open Letters Monthly, "...can reviews contribute to literary discussion something more lasting than a fleeing judgment based on 'taste' or inherently subjective standards?" Supplying an answer, he continues: "Domini's reviews demonstrate what would be lost if conscientious criticism disappeared."[1]

To which I'd add that his critical work deepens the conversation about literature (therefore, about culture, society, religion, politics), and that it does have importance or permanence. We get a good view of what his mind looks at and is jolted by when surveying the output of writers with an assortment of approaches. But the main thrust, as Domini states on the first page, is "an argument on behalf of latter-day non-traditional storytelling."

His persistence, and success, in promoting what might be called experimental or offbeat works depends, in large part, on the ability to reach back or out to some antecedent work or literary ancestor to shore up his case. The learning is worn lightly. Another sizeable part of Domini's appeal rests on style. While often plainspoken, there are the occasional fireworks and the intense involvement in the text under discussion. This earned him a predictable reprimand from the book's reviewer in *Publishers Weekly*: "Domini waxes poetic and philosophical... daring readers to find fault with his deep thoughts and complex tangents, and occasionally seeming a little too fond of his own voice when he attempts to turn even a simple review into an intellectual razzle-dazzle. He nevertheless upholds and defends his role as a reviewer and critic..."[2] Such dimness isn't surprising, and it's what we're often handed by criticasters—that writers shouldn't express themselves in a way that's fizzy and personable, they should submit competent, *colourless* reviews. And to top off Domini's sins, he actually "defends his role." Earlier I mentioned the pamphleteering aspect when it comes to wanting a book and its author to get noticed. Now it might be required to do the same for those critics who don't regurgitate the plot summary from the back of a book, slip in a half-baked criticism, and call it a day.

On finishing *The Sea-God's Herb* we might recall what Domini said at the beginning: "The more important point is that every critic gets his smart mouth smashed, sooner or later, by core quality. Remarks aren't literature, no matter how sharp the quip might look in a magazine. Remarks fall away and good work emerges..." That's an awareness any writer might want to keep in mind as a positive lesson, among many, from this worthwhile collection.

*

Anne of Tim Hortons: Globalization and the Reshaping of Atlantic-Canadian Literature, by Herb Wyile
TWR, 17 March 2012

Herb Wyile's new book on Atlantic-Canadian lit locates the reader "...not in a pastoral, romantic, pre-modern Maritime landscape but in a 'fallen' postmodern world of welfare apartments, tabloid violence, and doughnut shops–call it *Anne of Tim Hortons*." *Anne of Tim Hortons: Globalization and the Reshaping of Atlantic-Canadian Literature* is a diverting book that relies on carefully selected texts to show that the Folk of Atlantic Canada are being thoroughly commodified.

The novelists, playwrights, and poets Herb Wyile brings in to illustrate his points are engaged in addressing many serious issues: capitalism's overbearing and rapacious nature, resource-stripping, species-destruction, deforestation, pollution, out-migration, racism, sexism, and the replacement of trades and craftsmanship with tourism and a service economy. Add in the malignancy of Stephen Harper's "culture of defeat," the physical isolation from more cosmopolitan centres, an aging population, and chronic high unemployment, and one wonders how life goes on there at all.

According to Wyile, certain writers approach the current neoliberal and postcolonial context by undercutting smugly bland representations of history and weakening shoddy cultural foundations built by governments and tourism advocates. (Michelle Butler Hallett's *deluded your sailors*, which came out in November 2011, is too recent an example to be included in this work.) Among those receiving extended treatment, apart from other theoreticians and critics, are Michael Winter (*The Big Why*), Wayne Johnston (*The Colony of Unrequited Dreams* and *Baltimore's Mansion*), Charlie Rhindress (*The Maritime Way of Life*), George Elliot Clarke (*George & Rue*), Lisa Moore (*February*), and Alistair MacLeod (*No Great Mischief*). Wyile underlines how dominant a force Newfoundland and Labrador currently is in "highlighting the disparity between outsiders' expectations about life in the region and the more complicated and less idyllic lived realities of Atlantic Canadians."

Those negative aspects lead, in various ways, to a peculiar difficulty Atlantic-Canadian writers face. "That the cosmopolitanism of Atlantic-Canadian writing should come as a surprise, in other words, reflects the extent to which the region has been constructed as insular, primitive, effectively lost in time." However, "cosmopolitan" isn't how one reviewer of *Anne of Tim Hortons* sees matters: "One consequence of this approach [Wyile's emphasis on neo-liberalism and post-colonialism] is that the books selected are rarely those of the greatest artistic distinction," Steven Henighan wrote in "Guerillas or Folklorists?" (*Literary Review of Canada,* October 2011), which is beside the point, for Wyile has chosen texts that support his argument. No surprise there. Henighan is equally selective when he writes that while the "rest of us floated off into ersatz internationalism, Atlantic-Canadian writers, the country fiddlers of our literary scene, satisfied our nostalgic longing for authenticity and tradition."

It's a sign of the grimness of Wyile's book that one walks away from it in a melancholy mood, for the few positive finds—such as the very existence of Atlantic-Canadian literature, which I guess is at best a subset of Canadian literature—only augment the gloom. What he holds out hope for is that the variety of plays, poems, and especially the historical novel under discussion potentially will leave their readers wiser, and stiffen their spine for the long fight against entities like mining giant Vale, governments, hydroelectric companies, and the capital that sustains them. It sounds like wishful thinking to me; money being the sinew of affairs, a wad of paper doesn't stand much chance.

In remarks on David Adams Richards that appear early on,

Wyile states that, like a spirit (in his term, *éminence grise*), "…Richards hovers at the edges of this book somewhat uneasily. He has been vocal in emphasizing the primacy of moral and spiritual concerns in his writing, and, indeed, his work does not fit that readily with the kinds of political, social, and economic considerations driving this study…" A reader becomes aware that, admirable within its limits as Wyile's work is, missing from it are two key factors when considering writing: religion (or faith) and aesthetics. A third, not necessarily important in the context of Richards' concerns, is the dependency of publishers on subsidies, which I'll address first.

Relying as they do on provincial government funding, publishers feel threatened if it's removed, as was almost the case for PEI's Acorn Press in 2011. The reading public, a portion of Wyile's Folk, have a liking for this or that sort of story, and publishers aim to supply the required product, made by local hands, which both helps them get the grants to supply more of the same, and encourages other writers to design books that appease publisher, government, and the marketplace. In Newfoundland and Labrador when I was growing up, this meant the prevalence of rank works by "Uncle Al" Clouston and Ray Guy, while whatever might have been literary was not encouraged. Folk yarns sold well, and only recently are writers there building on other writing instead of oral tales.

Religion matters to people at the most private level, and at the most public (such as what political parties Catholics and Protestants traditionally voted for); how a denominational school system united and divided people; how those from other religions are regarded when they move to this region; and how the behavior of priests and Christian Brothers over decades (and here I don't mean only crimes against children) have influenced and shaped thought and policy, and formed part of the power structure. To not address religion is to leave out much of the fabric of a community that is considered important (whether one believes in something or rebels against it), maybe especially in the case of Newfoundland and Labrador.

Perhaps that's why Wyile is made uneasy by the shade of Richards. "Capitalism does not ask, What's the economy for? It merely asks it to grow," writes Curtis White in *The Barbaric Heart*, a sharp criticism of our current system. "The Barbaric Heart [an "ethical perspective" on capitalism] is a pure emptiness, an emptiness that doesn't know itself as empty. It is an emptiness that has turned upon itself. It is a moral black hole." *Anne of Tim Hortons* avoids that moral black hole, and thus removes itself from being an urgent document. I'm not going to suggest what Wyile should have done, but it's fair to say that what he didn't do was look dead on at the moral component of one of his topics.

When it comes to aesthetics, this book resolutely shies away from declaring that a novel is good or bad or inferior. The roaring of those "political, social, and economic" engines largely has drowned out the poetry and the craft of the writers Wyile has chosen. He does a good job elucidating novels and plays (a welcome aspect) on the topics that concern him, but do these books have intrinsic properties that make them Art? The books chosen, or at least some of them, took effort on the part of the writer as he or she fashioned a sentence. By leaving out the aesthetic qualities of the books under consideration, and concentrating on class, race, gender issues, and consumerism, Wyile leaves untouched a pertinent question: If the books aren't artful, how will they do whatever he wants them to do? They might as well be tracts left to molder on a doorstep. Wyile's earnestness, coupled with his thesis, tells the reader little about the literary aspect of literature. But it's fair for Wyile to have his preferences.

Instead of being content with what's been published, Wyile hands out a list of topics writers of the region could address:

Whether it is the history of absentee landlords on Prince

Edward Island, the history of the turbulent coal industry in Cape Breton, or even regional economic development in New Brunswick... there is certainly ample material for the kind of rich revisionings of the past that have become a staple of Canadian literature over the last four decades. As more and more writers come to resist the vision of the Maritimes as "a place that didn't count any more," we are likely to see in the literature of the region an increasingly varied, sophisticated, and inventive engagement with the past.

In the acknowledgments Wyile states that his "interest in Atlantic-Canadian literature" began in grad school and increased with conferences and papers. It's quite telling that deepening sophistication is predicated on further resistance to a stereotype, and ends there. Little is said about the aesthetic and emotional dimensions of a work and its receptivity, and repetition of themes is advised instead of the joy of freshness of subject and approach. What dominate are the above-mentioned grimness and an austere imagination. To those who expect writing to contain and embrace such things as compassion, experimentation, and inventiveness, *Anne of Tim Hortons* will come across as narrow and stingy, and in its focus and prescriptions a diversion from the deepest purposes of art. Herb Wyile's image of a doughnut quoted at the opening applies to his work: the big hole in his view of Atlantic-Canadian writing is where aesthetics and morality ought to be, as both are vital to a more complete understanding of the writers and readers of the region.

*

"A realm forever beyond reach": Steinbeck and Solzhenitsyn as presences in William Vollmann's *Expelled from Eden* and *Poor People*
EBR, 22 January 2008

In 2007 I asked Electronic Book Review if they'd like a review of a recent Vollmann book. The conversation resulted in a much longer work, and a much more enjoyable one to write, than the original plan, thanks to EBR's Joseph Tabbi and, especially, Stephen Burn. Many thanks to both. The annual talk of which US novelist deserves the Nobel usually begins with Philip Roth. Why not Vollmann instead? Is it his involvement with prostitutes that makes him, like Henry Miller, not respectable for consideration?

Introduction
It's a cliché to begin an essay on William Vollmann with a description of how much he has written. So let me begin with a quotation from a 1991 letter he wrote his publishers concerning other matters: "If *The Ice-Shirt* didn't make you money, *Fathers and Crows* isn't likely to make you money, either. Some of the *Dreams* set in the present may do better for you commercially. But *Seven Dreams* is not like a Stephen King book and will never be. I honestly believe that *Fathers and Crows* is my best work so far, and that it will eventually be recognized as such. In the meantime my other books, such as *Rainbow Stories*, are already recognized, and will only sell better as my name becomes better known." These lines appear in the last paragraph of "Letter Against Cuts," one of many heretofore unseen pieces of writing included in *Expelled from Eden: A William T. Vollmann Reader*, edited by Larry McCaffery and Michael Hemmingson (Thunder's Mouth Press, 2004).

The National Book Award-winning *Europe Central* (2005) followed *Rising Up and Rising Down* (2003), a seven-volume, 3,300-page study of violence in McSweeney's limited edition

29

(Ecco published a one-volume abridged version in 2004). Both have attracted attention and many reviews; the NBA has possibly brought newly curious readers to Vollmann. There is, as well, a certain cachet for any publisher to have this award-winning (in US literary circles) writer in their stable. So it seems that Vollmann prophesized correctly. In between those two major works came this *Reader*, and one may legitimately wonder how it solidifies his current reputation and position, where it situates him, and whether it's needed or premature.

Maturation

McCaffery addresses that second point. "The American literary scene that Vollmann entered in the late eighties... was going through a down period. Wishing to distance itself from the first wave of postmodernist experimentalism but unsure of how to define itself once this separation was made, it seemed to be suffering the effects of an extended hangover." With an apt disregard for nicety, Vollmann describes the lay of the land in "American Writing Today: Diagnosis of a Disease" (1990):

In this period of our literature we are producing mainly insular works, as if all our writers were on an airplane in economy seats, beverage trays shading their laps, faces averted from one another, masturbating furiously. Consider, for instance, The *New Yorker* fiction of the past few years, with those eternally affluent characters suffering understated melancholies of overabundance. Here the Self is projected and replicated into a monotonous army which marches through story after story like deadly locusts. Consider, too, the structuralist smog that has hovered so long over our universities, permitting only games of stifling breathlessness. (The New Historicism promises no better.)

He then gives seven points, or "rules," which will improve the state of the art. Two are of note here: "3. We should portray important human problems," and "7. *We should aim to benefit others in addition to ourselves*" (Vollmann's italics).

In a jaunty introduction that plays off Springsteen and pop culture in amusing ways, McCaffery says that Vollmann's *You Bright and Risen Angels* (1987) and *The Rainbow Stories* (1989) signaled that a new voice, full of energy and invention, had appeared in the land. Perhaps inevitably, he was declared the new Pynchon, though not at all reclusive, the only one who could write a book "like *Gravity's Rainbow*, which blew you away with its vast scope and ambition, erudition, intellectual brilliance, and story-telling skills, while opening up new areas for the novel as an art form." In the republic of US fiction, Pynchon is the Absent Prime Mover, and even literary atheists are forced to argue about his influence. A note tells readers that punk writer Kathy Acker was "a far more important figure during this period than Pynchon..."—though this will not satisfy those who believe that Pynchon's works, like Joyce's, saturate the atmosphere and cannot but be breathed in—akin to science fiction at an earlier period of Vollmann's life. The ongoing *Seven Dreams* sequence owes as much to the material and impressions Vollmann has gathered in travels to far-flung places as it perhaps does to the writers who he considers "contemporary" ("I'll assume you mean from the last two hundred years," he replied when McCaffery asked, in 1990, which contemporary authors he "admired"), including many who wrote multi-volume works or sequences, such as Mervyn Peake, Marcel Proust, Yukio Mishima, Sigrid Undset, André Malraux, James Blish, and Lawrence Durrell.

With 13 books out at the time the *Reader* was published, the third point—its need or presumption—can be answered in the affirmative. *Poor People* came out in 2007, and 2008 has already seen the appearance of a non-fiction work about life on trains—*Riding Toward Everywhere*—and may yet include a book on Noh plays, with *Imperial*, another non-fiction work about California, still to come. Not yet 50, Vollmann has many productive years left, which could mean that in five years it would be even more difficult to select what to put between two covers than it must have been. The editors and Vollmann haven't jumped the gun of posterity. With *Europe Central*'s award status, new readers can turn to the *Reader* as a handy reference work for what he's been thinking up to now. Since some of his books are hard to find, and others might seem off-putting due to the subject matter (prostitution or war), the *Reader* is a useful book for those who want to see what to choose next. Apart from offering novel samples, it includes segments from *Rising Up and Rising Down*, correspondence, and sizeable portions of the journalism that has put Vollmann in the way of bullets, landmines, drug lords, and the Taliban. Those already familiar with his work will be glad to see gathered up previously published essays and articles that appeared in this and that magazine, as well as previously unpublished material. McCaffery's introduction puts Vollmann and his writing in context, there's an amusing chronology that ends in 2010, and informative notes at the head of each excerpt.

Any *Reader*, once the last page is turned, makes us reflect on two things: what lay behind the selection process; and where the author started out and where he is now. So we come to the second point: what this does for and what it says about Vollmann's position. One could work against the editors' arrangement to see how Vollmann has changed over the years. Certainly his obsessions and concerns have remained constant, though some receive more attention at different periods. (Calling to mind what the narrator of Gilbert Sorrentino's *Imaginative Qualities of Actual Things* says: "Do you think for a moment that an artist selects his theme? It is all simple obsession..."[3]) The editors "wanted a collection that expanded the notion of what a literary reader might be... something akin to what's involved when a curator at a big museum mounts the first major retrospective of a particularly significant new artist." To do this, they arranged the Show according to themed section headings which are, in order, "Background and Influences"; "On Death, War, and Violence"; "On Love, Sex, Prostitutes, and Pornography"; "On Travel"; and "On Writing, Literature, and Culture." Appendices follow. This structure means that one can follow Vollmann's evolution of thought, and growth (which here means deepening and also growing away from). As one goes through the *Reader*, it becomes obvious Vollmann didn't begin as either a transgressive writer or an experimental writer—whatever those terms actually mean; with so many of both around who are distinguished from each other, surely finer distinctions are necessary—but as an exploratory one, at times naïve (*An Afghanistan Picture Show*, 1992), delving into subcultures and lives that most people insulate themselves from, such as criminal gangs and prostitutes. Speaking to Madison Smartt Bell in 1994, Vollmann described how he met some young men whom he hoped would teach him about "surfing on the tops of elevator cars; instead, however, these youths held him down and pressed lighted cigarettes into his arms."[4] What did he expect would happen?, one wonders. Never inclined to waste material, Vollmann used this experience to provide depth to scenes of death and self-mutilation by fire among the Iroquois in *Fathers and Crows* (1994).

That the arrangements of a variety of similar pieces don't bore one, as one sometimes feels when reading parts of either of John Barth's *Friday* books (which contain much that is entertaining and enriching), is due to the variety of writing styles as well as Vollmann's maturation in thinking. "On Travel," to consider briefly a short section, moves from pieces on Antarctica and Africa to "The Advantages of Space (1978)," a letter written by the 18-year-old writer to the physicist Freeman Dyson who wanted to set up colonies in space. It contains the idea that "perhaps some of us could set up something on asteroids or comets in a couple of decades..." One year later Vollmann is writing to the government of Saudi Arabia, proposing that as raw resources will become more slender on Earth, the asteroids between Mars and Jupiter could be mined. "The outlay will certainly be large, and transportation costs will also be high." He offers to "mine the asteroids for you," and ends with the touching: "Please write if you would like any elaboration." From someone who didn't have Vollmann's subsequent career of trekking to hostile places, this would seem only ludicrous. The very immodesty of the proposal, no matter how well-mannered the prose, in no way hides the earnestness. The next piece, "Subzero Debt, 1991," from *The Rifles*, shows a marked transition into a grown-up and finely balanced tone. The narrator, Vollmann in third-person, is in danger of freezing to death as he battles intense cold, an inadequate sleeping blanket, and stoves that will not heat properly. "He composed his epitaph: *I died for the advancement of Vapor Barrier Liners.*" Later he realizes that "if need be he could burn down all the buildings for warmth, one at a time!" That one exclamation mark catches everything—the desperate jokiness dire circumstances brings up in us, the evident satisfaction at such an idea, and the misery.

What follows that study in white and cold is "The Water of Life," an excerpt from *Imperial*, where Vollmann takes a raft journey down the poisonous New River (Rio Nuevo), which flows into the Salton Sea. He wants to go down this river that, apparently, no one has explored. He meets an ex-Marine named Jose Lopez. "When I told him nobody seemed willing to take me on the New River or even to rent me a rowboat, he proposed that I go to one of those warehouse-style chain stores that now infested the United States and buy myself an inflatable dinghy. I asked whether he would keep me company, and he scarcely hesitated. –Anyway, he said, it will be something to tell our grandchildren about." The voyage is hazardous, not least because the course of the river is unknown in some stretches. "And now another splash from Jose's paddle flew between my lips, so that I could enter more deeply into my New River researches. (How did it taste? Well, as a child I was given to partake of the sickly-salty Salk polio vaccine—an ironic association, I suppose, for one of the thirty-odd diseases which lives in the New River is polio.)" At journey's end Vollmann takes a shower but his hands continue to burn. "A week later, my arms were inflamed up to the elbow and my abdomen was red and burning. Well, who knows; maybe it was sunburn." In the introduction, McCaffery says "no other author has emerged with the talent and the drive and crazed sense of self-assurance that propels one on a flat-out, all-cylinders-burning, literary joy-ride," which is what one sees very clearly in this section, and equally in others.

What Vollmann has done is to keep moving and keep stretching himself. This is clearly evident in the *Reader*. He starts with Afghanistan and youthful idiocy, moving from there to San Francisco's prostitutes with his touching trust that using their drugs won't kill him, then through the history of North America in the *Seven Dreams* sequence, on into Thailand, where he frees a sex slave, war zones, and finally, in this selection, the murderous machinery of Germany and the Soviet Union in the 20th century. It's a trip that has its stumbles, and some of the material is not as interesting as one would wish it to be. But the unexpected is around every corner. When I read Vollmann, I think of a possible spiritual godfather, Blaise Cendrars (1887–1961). That remarkable sport, not a member of any -ism or clique, was born in Switzerland, and travelled the world (North and South Americas, Europe, Russia, and, self-myth has it, China). He may have written the first Modernist poem after returning to France in 1912. Cendrars joined the Foreign Legion to fight in the First World War for France, his adopted country, and lost his right arm (his writing arm). This didn't stop him from producing poetry, novels, essays, art criticism, journalism, and memoirs, or partici-pating in the film industry. While Vollmann regularly gets compared to David Foster Wallace and Richard Powers, perhaps critics might start looking elsewhere, and Cendrars is certainly one candidate.[5]

Many have commented on Vollmann's attachment to prostitutes. Janet Maslin, in a review of *Poor People*, referred to this feature of his writings: "As his devotees have come to expect, many of these tantalizingly spare settings involve prostitutes or drugs."[6] You don't need to be a columnist to figure out that most prostitutes don't enjoy a sybaritic lifestyle, or to ask what kind of setting she expects them to be in. And what, exactly, is tantalizing about such surroundings? We're left to puzzle that out while Maslin moves closer to the border of criticaster territory. After writing about prostitutes in three paragraphs in a review of 13 paragraphs, she can say: "The trouble with Mr. Vollmann's interest in whores..." without self-awareness.

In "The Shame of It All" (1999) Vollmann says this about prostitutes: "I have worshiped them and drunk from their mouths; I've studied at their feet. Many have saved me; one or two I've raised up. They've cost me money and made me money. People might say that we've 'exploited' each other. Some have trusted me; a few have loved me—or at least said so. They've healed my loneliness, infected me with diseases and despair." Again, from his conversation with Bell: "When I first began writing, I knew that my female characters were very, very weak and unconvincing, and I thought, what's the best way to really improve that? The best way is to have relationships with a lot of different women. The best way to do that is to pick up whores." Those who believe, like Maslin, that Vollmann never has moved on, or outward, from an unhealthy "interest in whores" would come away from the *Reader*, or reading his works, with a very different impression. The down-and-out who crowd Vollmann's early work are set alongside the Taliban and other armed and dangerous men, such as George W. Bush. As the novels and journalism go on, his interests have expanded to social issues such as the history of violence, wars, and environmental concerns, present in his fiction and non-fiction. "I'm actually a competent war correspondent at this point, instead of being a war idiot like I was in Afghanistan," he told Bell in 1994, and a similar progression can be seen in other areas. The *Reader's* arrangement of material hides this, though, with its thematic arrangement.

Vollmann's writing is warm and engaged, and he often subjects his beliefs to his sense of humour. An essay on writing begins with reflections on its physical toll. "I write this by hand, with swollen and aching fingers... While there have been occasions when I could not close my hand around a water-glass or turn the pages of a book, mostly this pain is an unobtrusive companion, a chronic irrelevance when I am loving my work, a chronic warning when I am not... pain always gives the same advice, the wisdom of prudes and legislators: stay within the limits." That last line is a typically smart turn of phrase and perception. He moves on to consider how the joy of writing has been transformed over the years. "I no longer feel, as I did at seventeen or twenty, that I am an ecstatic vessel bubbling over with words... I labor where before I played. In part this change is due to the pain in my hands." Vollmann considers the pleasures he's known, such as being by an ocean in Asia, or in the Arctic, which leads him to wonder if his work has lasting value compared with the examples of De Sade, "Hans and Sophie Scholl going to the scaffold for writing anti-Nazi pamphlets," or Joan of Arc: "...I hope never to be tested as they were. I know that I love what I do. I hope that my life (for which I give thanks) glides on and on, and that, like a good prostitute, I can continue to convert joy into cash."

That unexpected last line may provoke laughter, since many artists consider themselves prostitutes now and then. What was funny at the end of the essay about his hands ('hand job' springs to mind) here becomes ambiguous, or perhaps is how Vollmann sees the social contract between a writer and an audience. Not anything cold or sordid, but a recognition of human needs, human desires, and social commerce that happens to contains monetary value. Nothing highfalutin' about it.

Ambition

Generally, *Readers* don't make much of an impact, unless they're considered historically important. "It's hard to imagine Faulkner's ascendancy as Nobel Prize winner and 'American Shakespeare,'" wrote James Gibbons in his *Bookforum* review of *Expelled from Eden*, "without the catalyst of Malcolm Cowley's *Portable Faulkner*," which is "the gold standard for single-author anthologies because... [an author's] work needs to be 'opened up,' to be made accessible and intelligible without diminishing the allure of its mysteries, and that is precisely what Cowley achieved in his collection."[7] These are high standards, for Vollmann and his editors. Gibbons then states that of "contemporary authors, perhaps no one deserves a retrospective anthology at midcareer" as does Vollmann. So we can see that something hangs in the balance.

This "digestible abstract" of Vollmann's career "is a useful and often surprising" introduction which does not measure up to "unreasonable" expectations, as Gibbons acknowledges, that the *Reader* could do what Cowley's did. "By amassing such a vast bibliography in less than two decades, Vollmann has probably denied himself the readership he might otherwise have enjoyed." We're not in Cowley's golden age, when the audience for literature was larger and had more time to read long works in a leisurely fashion. Gibbons' point is taken, that any book, let alone a *Reader*, is going to face an uphill battle.

While McCaffery and Hemmingson's "palpable enthusiasm" is appreciated, their editing principles irritate Gibbons. After criticism of the 'slackness' of the head notes, and that line drawings from one of the *Seven Dreams* novels aren't presented along with the excerpt, Gibbons turns to the lack of Vollmann's "source notes," which he argues are vital to the books themselves and could have been replicated in some instances. These are cavils; by nature, an anthology must leave some things out. As to sloppiness, nowadays few publishers seem to employ proofreaders. There is definitely more substance to the charge that since the "editorial apparatus... takes up a good fifth" of the reader the editors could have limited their own words and allowed in more of Vollmann's.

Often Vollmann's writing and travel have been fuelled by writing assignments for magazines, yet he has a sensible and probably self-protective disdain for how his pieces are treated by editors. This is made clear in the *Reader*. He puts up with the cuts, and makes the case that he can restore the passages in future books "someday." Not necessarily this one. Gibbons points out that the editors, presumably with Vollmann's assent, have chosen to go with the edited versions of pieces, despite having the freedom to print the original. However, if the original of some piece was longer, then using the shorter version is justified if it allows more space for other material.

Writing on the *Reader* and *Europe Central* for the *New York Review of Books*, Michael Wood makes a point similar to Gibbons': "There is a slightly awkward irony too in so much room being given to the writer's letters to his editors protesting cuts in his *Seven Dreams* novels; we could have been reading some of the stuff Vollmann didn't want to cut."[8] We return to McCaffery's explanation of the vision behind the *Reader*—"We wanted a collection that expanded the notion of what a literary reader might be"—and continue with Wood's review: "But then this collection, addressed to the 'astute Vollmann reader, scholar, fan, and fanatic,' is not meant to introduce anyone to Vollmann... Everyone reading it will already have read him. Well, nearly everyone." If that's true—impossible to verify, or dispute—then what for Wood is "awkward irony," viewed from another angle, provides a glimpse into a different part of the mind behind the books. In "Crabbed Cautions of a Bleeding-hearted Un-deleter—and Potential Nobel Prize Winner" (1998), a letter to Paul Slovak of Viking, Vollmann declares: "This sounds crazed and immodest, but I actually believe I have a shot at winning the Nobel Prize or some other prestigious award someday. If Viking sticks with me that long, I think they may benefit from keeping me happy and by keeping the books intact. I am also getting more and more foreign sales these days. May the company please, please, just be patient." This can be seen as self-puffery, but that doesn't show itself in any other instance—when he's in a war zone, as an example—where he could easily make himself out to be heroic. It comes across as earnest, the same earnestness behind those letters about mining asteroids, and might be what Wood calls "innocence." The letter could also be an honest plea covering the hint of a threat. The ambitious writer (ambitious for his art) may be saying to Viking that they ought to keep him happy because, after all, he could move somewhere else. That ambition, and the earnestness, is evident in his books; so too is the awkwardness, seen in Vollmann as a creative writer, journalist, and correspondent. This vein runs through him, and showing it is, in part, what has gained him his readership and helped him make his art.

Any *Reader* that isn't selective risks becoming narrow and monotonous. Yet Wood comes across as obtuse when he says the shortness of the extracts doesn't align with "the pace and space of Vollmann's work." Surely Vollmann doesn't always need to stretch out in the literary equivalent of a railway station. (Or an airplane's Business-Class seats, to return to his metaphor from above.) He is economical and terse when he chooses to be. Wood closes his dual review by writing of *Europe Central* that "the great virtue of his writing is that even at its windiest it tries to think with us rather than for us," an observation borne out by the reading process. One follows (sometimes with disbelief) what Vollmann is saying about pornography or his wrists, and it seems like the sentences spring up of their own accord, without much premeditation; they possess a liveliness and unexpectedness that can convince the reader she is discovering what Vollmann is discovering or feeling at almost the same time as he does.

I find it peculiar, though, when Wood says the *Reader* doesn't allow us to "get much sense of the more thoughtful writer," preferring to emphasize "Vollmann's energy and eccentricity," which matches Gibbons when he writes "…the Reader serves as surrogate autobiography, a patchwork of memoir… that shed light on his core beliefs…" What captures readers of Vollmann's novels and journalism may very well be his own presence (and yet he's not quite there, since he uses substitutes), which is a thoughtful, patient person who places himself in situations "safety nazis and safety monkees"[9] would tut-tut over. While in the *Reader* we don't get long stretches of uninterrupted chains of thought, we do get to see many different links. In his *Times Literary Supplement* review of the unabridged *Rising Up and Rising Down*, Paul Quinn made the worthwhile point that the reader is aware of "the mental and physical labour behind the work which does not destroy the mystique of the art, but draws the reader into its making with great intensity."[10] I wonder if it's this intensity, brought about by prolonged immersion in any one of his books, which Wood and Gibbons miss most and which no *Reader* could satisfy.

Many reviewers (such as Gibbons) discuss at length Vollmann's willingness to place himself in harm's way. He wants to see what's going on and come to his own conclusions; he does not want to be a hero, or a Hemingway. This is most apparent in the section "On Death, War, and Violence" which, among other things, shows him interviewing a member of the Japanese Yakuza ("Regrets of a Schoolteacher," 1998) and, in "Across the Divide" (2000), back in Afghanistan. Vollmann waits to meet the Minister of the Interior, and encounters many Talibs. "When the interview was over, I gave a chocolate bar to the dirtiest, hungriest-looking one of them. He was wearing a T-shirt that said 'Oakland Raiders.' When I told him that the Oakland Raiders were American, he was crestfallen, and the others all laughed at him." Vollmann doesn't. He works to maintain respect for those many of us would turn away from. *Books in Canada* reviewer Matt Sturrock, considering *Poor People*, where Vollmann discusses beggar women in Afghanistan, regards this attitude as a flaw. "In other places, however, the culture-specific proprieties and courtesies he has picked up through extensive travel seem to have overmastered his moral sense. Vollmann's reluctance to condemn the Talibs for their abominable oppression of Afghanistan's women is a failure on his part."[11] In *Rising Up and Rising Down* Vollmann said: "Do I betray and humiliate those who have trusted me, or do I soften my conclusions? My policy will always be to treat with empathy and respect anyone agreeing to be studied, interviewed, exposed. I would have been courteous to Eichmann. My obligation, however, is to the truth."[12] One can argue with him on this point, and it is no small matter. Yet the attempt to be empathetic, while determined to try and get to the core of matters, is particularly significant at a time when his country's government has worked steadily to make those not pro-US—Taliban, Iraqis, North Koreans, Cubans, Old Europeans, Canadians, Mexican immigrants—one vast Other to be denigrated, feared, reviled, and condemned.

In "Some Thoughts on the Value of Writing During Wartime" (2002–2003) Vollmann presents his viewpoint on the Second Gulf War in moderate language:

I can only speculate on our President's real motives in determining to remove [Saddam Hussein]. It can't be his murderousness, because the United States, like most powerful countries, has allied itself with butchers many times before and is doing so now. The reason may be Saddam's dangerousness to American citizens or interests, but so far our

President has given us, and the rest of the world, no hard facts about that. It is as if we read a Raymond Chandler novel which simply asserted, rather than proved, that a certain person were the killer. I think we'd feel a little disappointed. I myself am not necessarily against invading Iraq, if our government can do us the courtesy of making a decent explanation.

In times of upheaval, extreme positioning, and censorship (self-imposed or demanded), it takes some courage to speak like this. It may not seem as daring as venturing to the Arctic, but throughout *Expelled from Eden* we come to see Vollmann as fearless (or reckless) in different fashions. I'll return to this point when discussing *Poor People*.

The *Reader* ends two ways: first, and most importantly, with "Steinbeck: Most American of Us All" (from *Imperial*). Here we are re-introduced to sentiments voiced in "Some Thoughts on Neglected Water Taps," a piece from 2000 about Deep Springs College (where Vollmann was a student), that contains the pregnant thought he had while there: "We ought to identify and empathize with the physical and moral order of the universe, whatever that may be, and we should help others do the same," preceded by a lesson wrapped in a question: "What if I could go out and do good?" This goes in a straight line to Steinbeck, who "wanted all of us to be angry and sorry about the plight of the Okies, and his own outrage is what makes *The Grapes of Wrath* a great book." Outrage, doing good, and actions for others; these motivations are present throughout Vollmann's work. From here it's useful to turn once more to the rules which come at the end of the already quoted "American Writing Today: Diagnosis of a Disease." Rule 3, again: "We should portray important human problems." Rule 1 reads, "We should never write without feeling." Rule 7, repeated from above, says, "*We should aim to benefit others in addition to ourselves*" (Vollmann's italics). The anger Vollmann admires in Steinbeck is a positive force; it can be used for social and aesthetic good; the same is as true for Vollmann. The drowning of his sister when he was supposed be watching over her has governed many of his rescues and engagements with the world, but literature generally—here represented by Steinbeck—gave shape, and Deep Springs provided training, for the transformation of his socially inclined earnestness into deeds. "I want to take some responsibility and act as well as write, do things that'll help people somehow, things like kidnapping the sex slave," Vollmann told Bell. After winning the NBA for *Europe Central* he said that when he understood he was "partly German" he asked himself if he was guilty for what had happened in the Second World War.[13] *Rising Up and Rising Down*, most notably in its Moral Calculus, is another manifestation of this desire to engage with world problems.

Expelled from Eden ends the second time with Appendix D, "CoTangent Press Book Objects," an overview of small books done in limited editions with drawings and watercolours by Vollmann. We've come through his exhaustive, ambitious, intricate novels and intensely engaged journalism to wind up at images of items of beauty, handmade works he has devised, as if he's saying: If you want proportion and delicacy, then here, I can do that. Chamber music, after his own Ring.

Culmination

Perhaps the *Reader* ended too quietly. While it charted Vollmann's deep involvement with counter-cultures, violence, drugs, sex, and war, it did make clear that he had moved out of those circles and had turned to other interests. This may have been seen as a retreat from outrage into niceness and domesticity. Maybe he had simply grown weary or complacent. "Conservatism is our opposition... It's evenings, when I'm somewhat played out, when I'm likely to be most conservative," Charles Fort declared in *Wild Talents*. "Everything that is highest and noblest in my composition is most pronounced when I'm not good for much. I may be quite savage, mornings: but, as my energy plays out, I become nobler and nobler, and lazier, and conservativer..."[14] The energies of a young man are usually required to keep outrage fresh. *Rising Up and Rising Down* aside—it had been written over "twenty-three years" as of 1998 (*Expelled from Eden*)—perhaps Vollmann had become disenchanted with the arduous life, as demonstrated by this assessment of his physical state in *Poor People*: "My visual memory has deteriorated since I suffered a series of minor strokes..." Anything could have brought on the strokes—drug use, mines exploding, stress, diseases that weakened his constitution. But the statement is said without self-pity or regret. It just is. What people have come to expect from Vollmann—the hazardous journeys outwards and inwards, enduring hardships commensurate with travel (political and otherwise)—might not appeal any more to a man approaching his half-century and enjoying a wife and daughter, and some success.[15]

Writers are not beholden to anyone to do anything when it comes to searching for inspiration. They can retire into affluent silence, take up Noh theatre[16], write as little as possible—or they can join the "schizophrenic or alcoholic" hobos (Seaman, *Bookforum*) found on railroad cars. Another writer might repeat himself, but for *Poor People*, Vollmann gathered together notes from earlier travels and made fresh excursions to discuss the plight of the poor of the world. He didn't have only Okies in mind.

The Solzhenitsyn Reader may seem like an inappropriate text to place alongside Vollmann's recent works. At first glance it seems improbable that there would be any similarity between an almost 90-year-old believer in the Orthodox Church and Vollmann. Without insisting too much on the point—for there are many differences—I'd like to suggest that the earnestness, integrity, artistic intent, and social activism seen in Vollmann does echo some of the moral, religious, aesthetic, and political concerns found in Aleksandr Solzhenitsyn, survivor of the Gulag, cancer, and life in the Soviet Union generally. In the Introduction to *Rising Up and Rising Down* Vollmann writes:

> They say that Soviet frontline officers in action against the Nazis thought that they had seen it all, but death in Stalin's prison camps was entirely a different sort of death. Solzhenitsyn was for eleven years a prisoner in those camps. He suffered, bore witness, had, one would think, the necessary experience. His account of the day-to-day struggle there, *One Day in the Life of Ivan Denisovich*, deserves our appalled respect. Yes, he can be called an authority, an expert.[17]

So it will be worthwhile to keep at the front of the mind certain concerns these two writers address.

Vollmann states: "I haven't *lived* in the mouth of violence; I've only paid a few visits" (*RURD*). In the Introduction to *Poor People* he is again straightforward: "I can fairly state that I have studied, witnessed and occasionally been a victim of violence. I cannot claim to have been poor. My emotion concerning this is not guilt at all, but simple gratitude." Similarly, in the closing section of the book he confesses, "I am a petty-bourgeois property owner." As a counter-text, Vollmann uses James Agee and Walker Evans' guilt-filled *Let Us Now Praise Famous Men*, which he slams as "an elitist expression of egalitarian longings... Its Communist sympathies, expressed, I am sad to say, in the midst of the Stalinist show trials, expose its naiveté..." (One can picture Solzhenitsyn nodding in agreement.) Agee "carries his sincerity to the point of self-loathing," while Evans "escapes into the tell-all taciturnity of photography... he need not commit himself." "Agee does commit himself," and it's no surprise that commitment is what Vollmann most appreciates, even if Agee and Evans talked over the heads of their subjects to the rich who most often will not "possess the desire" to read about such people. ("When [*Poor People*] is published I will give away several copies... to whomever then happens to be living in my parking lot.") Walter Kirn, who has some good things to say about Vollmann in the *New York Times*, rebuts that point: "Who but the rich can help the poor—or arrange things so they can more easily help themselves? And what does it matter if guilt moves them to do it?"[18] In fact, governments have a moral role to help the poor, and all sectors within their borders.

Consider Kirn's point in the light of what Solzhenitsyn said in his 1972 Nobel Lecture: "The salvation of mankind lies only in making everything the concern of all."[19] (Except for the word "salvation," with its religious connotation, that could almost be one of Vollmann's rules for writers.) That "all" means the rich, Kirn, you and me. If we lived in a shame culture, *Poor People* would change our perceptions of how we treat the indigent, the cast-offs, the shatterbrained and the preyed upon in such a way that the sentiment behind governments' feeble efforts to end child poverty would have its backbone stiffened. We don't live in that culture.

Those who pick up *Poor People* may set it down with a fuller, more compassionate heart, though that isn't Vollmann's aim. "This essay is not written *for* poor people, or for anyone in particular. All that I dare to do is to note several similarities and differences which I believe pertain to the experience of being poor." This could be viewed as a typical liberal's way of describing a problem without offering a solution. Over a period of years he interviewed the poor of various countries, including the US, Yemen, Mexico, Japan, Russia, Pakistan, Hungary, Afghanistan, and Kenya, starting with one question, "Why are you poor?" The answer led to further exchanges, which gave Vollmann information that he has turned into a living, breathing document—with occasional statistics (the validity of which he is suitably cautious about)—which is humane and affecting. However, the very act of setting out into the world and visiting poor people where they live (not necessarily at fixed addresses), asking that simple question, hearing the replies, and trying to make sense of them has rubbed two *New York Times* critics the wrong way. "[Vollmann] acts as if he were the Louis Pasteur of poverty, identifying its forms for the first time through the lens of some sociological microscope." Maslin believes "Mr. Vollmann" merely "assembles glimpses and anecdotes from many places and then creates simple truisms to unite them... *Poor People* feels like a collection of outtakes on which themes have been superimposed."

Those are two uncharitable assessments, and to reach those opinions requires deafness to Vollmann's modest voice. He presents tables of income which he does not trust, he states quite clearly the "impossibility of my gaining any dynamic understanding of these lives *over time*" (Vollmann's italics), and states that he can only "*show* and *compare*" (Vollmann's italics). He often criticizes himself for his own failures, his privileges, and his ability to walk away from poverty. I can't find anything that marks him as a sociologist or a Pasteur, nor do these testimonials seem like leftover pieces from earlier books. What those two readers may be missing is this: that the search for what poor people think and say about their lives has more priority for Vollmann than what he thinks, either in advance or after. There is not a single page that does not address, obliquely or directly, quietly, with outright anger, or in genuine sympathy, the predicament of the poor in such ways that readers are thrust into regarding their own actions when it comes to world poverty and neighborhood concerns.

Many reviewers have commented on the organization behind *Poor People*, and it's worth saying a few words about that. The book is broken into sections: Self-Definitions, Phenomena, Choices, Hopes, Placeholders, followed by sources, acknowledgements and roughly 100 photographs. (Maslin writes: "Mr. Vollmann took the book's raw, abrasive photographs himself, and he is most assuredly no Walker Evans." Here, one can ask: Who can be Evans except Evans? This, like her entire review, is snide and wrong-footed.) Looking more closely at the contents page, one can see that some chapters focus on one place and many roam all over the world. "...[I]ts rigor comes and goes," notes Maslin; "Structurally, the book is unevenly proportioned; chapter ten features content drawn from nine different countries over six time periods, while chapter sixteen, one of the longest, draws from just one,"[20] complains Sturrock, who in Masonic fashion is keeping to himself how many time zones a writer can traverse.

"It's not a systematic examination of poverty, and it's certainly not a treatise on how to respond to poverty... Mostly it's a pointillist description..." writes Nicholas Kristof, "perhaps closer to travel literature than poverty literature,"[21] which is very even-handed; "Vollmann circl[es] rhythmically around the problem of global poverty... The rest of the book spirals in ever-more complex gyres, integrating and adding information and complications as it proceeds."[22] There is something in that which, mixed with Kristof's remarks, comes as close as one can get to the book's structuring. Here it may be useful to consider what Paul Quinn noted in his review of *Rising Up and Rising Down*: "His fiction has always aspired to the essay: it is discursive, often employing an elaborate apparatus of endnotes and cross reference, quotation and bibliography."[23] Unless one wants to fruitlessly wish a peach to be an apple, then demanding organization from a "personal approach" that "makes the book bad science" (Munger[24]) is bound to disappoint.

Vollmann's writing style is full of nervy associative leaps (for all the surface calm here), and there's no telling what will happen next. We're meant to feel that we are in that mind, a few synapses behind, and compelled to follow. (This was noted with *Expelled from Eden* also.) On page 256 he's near a New York toilet, and on the next page, for only a few words, we're in the "filthy toilets" of Nairobi. We think like this, at times, but some writers have the ability to capture the jumps our minds make more effortlessly than others. It might be a theme that lures him, or the harmonies of answers to why people are poor; a conversation in a shelter with a woman named Mary brings to mind the Irish Famine. We're given impressions, not many hard facts, about the wandering lives of those who he sees once, maybe more, because this is all he knows about them. Vollmann doesn't pretend it's anything but that.

"I do not wish to experience poverty, for that would require fear and hopelessness." In order to get us as close to such states as possible, Vollmann offers case studies. To provide a baseline, so to speak, for comparisons throughout, in the first pages he relates the tale of Sunee (Thailand), a woman employed by a cleaning company, who lives with her mother and daughter. She is usually drunk or hoping to get a drink. She may have been a prostitute. "Can you change your destiny?" he asks, and she replies, "Impossible. Always poor." When he meets Wan, a beggar existing in the Central Railroad Station of Bangkok, confined to the streets and not able to live in Sunee's splendid shack that features a blue vinyl sheet covering the floor, Vollmann asks, "In your idea, why are some people rich and some poor?" This small, under-nourished, disease-spotted 23-year-old replies, "I think I am rich..." Being rich, like being poor, is relative. "I remember from Madagascar the gaping mouth and sad black eyes of the old beggar-lady who clutched with spider-boned hands at the skin that sagged from her bony face; she said that she could never remember filling her belly...; it would have been an insulting taunt to ask her if she were poor; her belly had answered me." (John Cowper Powys met a raggedly dressed tramp on a Welsh road in 1940 and handed him his scarf. Then, "pinching this ragged coat gingerly with finger and thumb," said "'how cold, how icy, you must be!'" to which the tramp replied "with an indifferent and detached air... 'I have a very warm singlet on.'"[25])

For 300 pages Vollmann presents us with stories, each dovetailing into other subjects, or amplifying what we've read before, the lone voice of Sunee swelling into a chorus, each story deepening the meaningfulness of answers to such twinned questions as "What is poverty? Who are the rich?" Wan thinks differently from Sunee, and her answers might please an economist with the World Bank. On another page we're in Sarajevo, in 1992, "when the deep sullen thumpings and almost happy firecracker-poppings of small-arms fire had fallen away..." Three people voice different opinions about the temporary, fraught silence. One is thankful, the second is immured within indifference, and the third says, about a fat man, "Anybody in Sarajevo who's fat is an asshole." For Vollmann this statement shows "class hatred at its clearest. Sarajevo's people were now divided into the (relatively) safe and the accident-prone, the well-fed and the hunger-pained—in short, the rich and the poor." Aren't the poor automatically, in many people's minds, less intelligent, because they evidently didn't apply themselves, and because being poor has never been smart?

But they can be temporarily useful. "To the extent that the poor constitute a supply of something—cheap labor, easy availability for some project (war or prostitution, for instance), convenient obedience—they will be tolerated, even 'wanted.' To the extent that they constitute a demand for common resources, they will be unwanted." That demand continues to grow, so only a hapless Pollyanna could believe the poor will ever be valued universally as human beings.

While in Hanoi, Vollmann has a friendly waitress, "smiling, lovely and young," who flirts with him. "Giggling, she asked whether I would marry her. I was not much younger than I am now and certainly no handsomer, so I might as well consider the possibility that to the extent that it truly attracted her to become my wife, financial calculations operated." At some point he notices Hong, a phrasebook seller positioned next to the restaurant, "and when I invited him to breakfast, I myself lost considerable matrimonial appeal in her eyes." The photographs illustrate the people he has met, as well as their frail accommodations, when they have any. Similar to when he has Hong join him for a meal, Vollmann places the poor, the citizenry of the world, in front of the reader, visually and anecdotally. In my case, they accompanied me on a flight to Iqaluit in the Canadian north. What do you do with those faces, showing a bewildering and wearying array of moods—hostile, manic, imploring, numbed, cautiously hopeful, lost in pleasure over a personal pursuit? The waitress' face "grew hideous with hatred." What face do we make in response?

One response among critics is boredom (possibly fatigue) and almost a chiding of Vollmann's pursuit. Kirn: "Vollmann's interview subjects, it turns out, explain their suffering in the same ways that most who suffer explain their suffering, especially when they're in the midst of it. It's fate. It's bad luck. It's punishment. And so on. Could nonpoliticians and noneconomists who are absorbed in the business of survival answer any other way?" Perhaps not. If all Vollmann did was classify the poor as interviewees and approach them with a short questionnaire, then he, and we, would never have heard about the complicated, fascinating, and at times fabricated life story of Natalia (Vollmann is courteously sceptical of her accounts, and persists in the search for truth from her, and from all the people he meets), and the more plain-spoken Oksana, two beggars in Russia. Without his larger purpose—to learn—he would not have met Oksana's daughter Nina and her family, including Nina's husband who had been exposed to radiation at Chernobyl.

Kristof's review discusses the repetitive answers voiced by the poor: "The problem is that the answers aren't very interesting, persuasive, or authoritative. It's useful to ask poor people about poverty, but after wading through three hundred pages of their equally impoverished answers, unleavened by some larger context or theme, I think Vollmann would have been better off spending some of his time asking such questions of a panel of Ivy League professors." In *Bookforum* Vollmann addressed this: "When you talk to poor people, you often meet people whose minds and spirits have been starved like their bodies, and so they're not capable of eloquence."[26] There is agreement that there is a "problem" with the answers, but from divergent perspectives, as Vollmann is not out to find the solutions Kristof would like to see.

When Kristof tries to discern Vollmann's motives his writing becomes ambiguous. "So we now have a wealth of interest in poverty. A fruit of that, or perhaps a beneficiary of it, is William Vollmann's new work..." It's not too far from Maslin's tone, revealed in her use of words and phrases such as "interestingly manipulative," "ostensible," "purports," and "coyness." Whatever is going on in Maslin, or Kristof, remains mysterious. On the contrary side, Sturrock honestly admits to a line drawn within his own soul: "[Vollmann] is unflappable and kind—traits exemplified in the chapter where he meets a Thai girl with a ghastly facial disfigurement. Of her, he says simply: 'And yet her smile was formed, her gaze distinctly her own. Were she my lover, I could very easily find her beautiful.' His generosity in that instance shamed this reader."[27]

As my airplane burned fuel over parts of Ontario, Quebec, and Nunavut, I read "Crime Without Criminals," a chapter that focuses on Kazakhstan in 2000. In this new country, several oil companies were "gainfully employed in exploiting what the consortium's press releases labeled *the world's deepest supergiant oil field*" (Vollmann's italics). The consortium is called Tengizchevroil (TCO for short). It's worth quoting all of the opening paragraph: "I'm going to tell you an ugly little story now, a story which sickens and shames me in my heart; but fortunately it takes place in a country most of us have never heard of, and, moreover, the saddest parts are all secondhand, without 'hard evidence,' so we might as well pretend that they're untrue." Not for the first time, Vollmann goes where even his drivers and interpreters refuse to go unless prodded. He heads to Sarykamys. On "TCO's highway" at night he sees this:

Well, even though it was already dark I now began to make out a sunset ahead... But ahead was to the south, not the west. And this sunset, orange and purple, was more like a bruise in the darkness than that customary celestial luminosity which tinges the sky all around itself; if anything, the darkness seemed heavier and puffier around this purple glow which now began to resolve itself into multiple fires... Plumes of smoke, plumes of fire! It was spectacular. But that smoke, how it crept and crawled and wriggled across the entire sky! TCO was doing its mite for global warming. That smoke would give the next generation another reason to curse us—two reasons, actually, for not only did it pollute the air and ground, it also burned off much of the fuel that was ostensibly being refined. Of course, a few members of the present generation would get rich.

Upon arriving in Sarykamys Vollmann tries to find out about environmental pollution and sickness—the sulfur fumes, and other chemicals contained in oil burn-off, may have affected people's health. Nurses refuse to answer his questions ("When they understood that I was a journalist, their despondent apathy gave way to fear"), so he visits the house of the doctor-in-chief.

She said that she had a temperature. She too was trembling now, just as both nurses had trembled, which is why I feel bad about telling you the name of the village, which really is Sarykamys, but even if that doctor and those nurses lose their jobs as a result of this story (which I sincerely hope that they won't), I must believe that what's most important is to tell the truth, for the sake of the four or five thousand inhabitants of Sarykamys whose health that doctor and those nurses ought to be protecting.

What is everyone afraid of? A venerable newspaperman later explains to Vollmann, "in small towns the old *atmosphere* of repression might well remain" (Vollmann's italics).

In closing his Nobel lecture, Solzhenitsyn repeated a Russian proverb: "One word of truth shall outweigh the whole world."[28] We may recall Vollmann's declaration in *Rising Up and Rising Down*, quoted above—"My obligation, however, is to the truth"—as well as Rule 6 from "American Writing Today: Diagnosis of a Disease": "We should believe truth exists" (*Expelled from Eden*). Getting to the truth among the poor (or any stratification of society), or about anything, is a constant aim in Vollmann's writings. Often in *Poor People*—as specified right off with the Income Table—it is practically impossible to determine, but that makes reaching for it an even more crucial ethical and moral imperative. It can't be called a defeat if there's never been an attempt. The suspicion with which post-modernist writers view what is said operates strongly in Vollmann. In "Some Thoughts on the Value of Writing During Wartime" he gives three pieces of advice to writers, of which the third is of note here: "In these times, any one of you who feels inclined to risk a little and learn a lot should travel to an Islamic country to make friends and to learn, not to teach... You should get to know them well enough to understand why what they believe is plausible to them, and you should explain their views to other Americans as sympathetically and as accurately as you can" (*Expelled from Eden*). What is plausible, not what is true, is sometimes the most we can know (though being satisfied with that isn't enough). Interrogation of circumstances and people is demanded.

Maslin calls the trip to Sarykamys "the book's boldest journey..." but then, as if regretting such praise, continues: "But we have been hearing a lot about Kazakhstan." Perhaps for that reason she doesn't mention anything about what Vollmann has presented. "Of course," he writes, "you and I are more guilty than [the people of Kazakhstan]. We create the demand for TCO's product, we pollute the atmosphere with it, and about Sarykamys we don't give a rat's ass. And if you disagree with me about your own responsibility, read this story to the end and then decide whether you would be willing to forgo your petroleum addiction for a single day." Maslins the world over have had a bellyful of this kind of chatter.

While reading about Sarykamys, I thought of any city or community where industry trumps basic health requirements and environmental controls. At 30,000 feet thanks to precious fossil fuel being burned, with flags being staked to the Arctic Ocean's seabed, and the continued possibility of Alaska's Arctic Wildlife Refuge being opened to oil, did I feel complicit? Yes. Was that Vollmann's purpose? As he says, we all have "some degree of moral freedom." Of course, his travel implicates him as well. He points fingers when he feels that's justified, but he never hectors. "This book is not 'practical.' It cannot tell anyone what to do, much less how to do it. For all I know, the *normality* of our epoch may render resource-sharing substantially impossible. But *what is greater or braver than to beat down misfortune*, or at least to try?" (Vollmann's italics.) We are left to our own ethical devices, just as Vollmann was left to his. We are asked to puzzle out for ourselves the questions he has posed. The norm in this case is that we rely on oil; and so does Vollmann to get where he's going. We must view the way things are from a variety of perspectives, and, by so doing, upend our habits of thought and behavior.

In the second-last chapter of *Poor People*, titled "I Know I Am

Rich," Vollmann describes a property he owns which has a parking lot that is home to the homeless. If "Crime Without Criminals" is the angriest chapter, this is the saddest. (One might be able to make the argument that these two chapters are pivots around which the rest of the material whirls.) It begins, Bob Slocum-style, with "I am sometimes afraid of poor people," and it describes how Vollmann allows the homeless to sleep on his property, but never lets them in the building. "Once in a great while there were thugs in my parking lot at night, men who were demanding, menacing and, from my petty-bourgeois perspective, insolent. I made a point of declining whatever they asked of me, but I spoke more politely to them than I wished, because I was afraid. Were they poor? They must have been poor in something, to entertain themselves in my parking lot..." He introduces his daughter to them "because I do not wish her to grow up disdainful of poor people or needlessly afraid of them." This introduction does not mean he is incautious. The blinds over the windows are "always drawn" and tinfoil has been taped over the insides.

The building has a steel door, likened to a door in Hanoi "which only kings could enter." Behind this, Vollmann hopes he is safe. "Might not the continued existence of my domain behind that steel door have been a perpetual offense and harm to Carty [one of the homeless]? It is true that his poverty eternally threatened my richness. But I defeated him again and again; every day I shut him out into the rain." The steel door is a necessity, and also a powerful metaphor. Perhaps Vollmann didn't intend to summon up Max Weber's iron cage (or steel shell) from *The Protestant Ethic and the Spirit of Capitalism*, but in a work devoted to the poor and the rich, it would not be out of place thematically.

However, the steel door's protection is not complete — "Sometimes I worry that they will come through the roof" — and it calls to mind those nervously cocooned inside gated communities. Vollmann treats the homeless on his parking lot with politeness and gifts: "...I will give them small things such as a bottle to get drunk or a little money." But then he looks at this giving of alms as potentially a service that reflects well on us. "Must charity satisfy me? It was not charity to give to the legless Serb; that was like giving to myself, moving money from one pocket to another." Also: "Again, must charity please me? Is it incumbent on me to feel a specific way, or do I so demand a certain standard from others? If it feels like charity, have I failed?"

Poor People is not a product of the UN, a think-tank or institute, but the result of one man's explorations of the responses to the question, "Why are you poor?" The outward reach of this book is undeniable, in my opinion, and not something each of his books succeeds in doing. (I find many parts of, as an example, *The Rainbow Stories* tiresome and uninteresting.) Others disagree, or ignore certain aspects of it, dwelling on faults in its organization or its limits (Vollmann's self-limitations, one could also say). Critical writing, or academic writing, works to explain how *Poor People* (and *Expelled from Eden*) doesn't work, or does work, or how Vollmann tries and succeeds at getting this or that right, falls down here and there, and so forth. These purposes have value at all times, but they are not the only values. Critical writing will rarely get anyone excited about a work, or be taken up by it, except, possibly, philosophically or as a text to be treated with theories. The excitement will be intellectual, but won't commit someone's blood and soul to the works, which Vollmann, with Steinbeck in mind, has written from the fibre of his being, as used to be said before the author supposedly disappeared.

So without that equal passion—or more accurately, any fervor save the excitement caused by intellectual analysis—how can anyone enter deeply where Vollmann has been to understand the tales he has dragged back for us to peruse in our living rooms and studies? How do we commit? It's not a condemnation to read him as writers, academics, or critics. But when he writes of prostitutes "in debt to the Yakuza," how can we keep in balance the aim of most explication—to stay detached—and an awareness of the miserable life led by "sad-eyed Czech and Russian girls"? We do, though, and while we do, we remove ourselves from the furnace of injustice. If we aren't in some way with Vollmann on that level, then we're regarding José González or a tuna fisherman in Yemen as text only. But they're not. Vollmann delves into their lives, for shorter or longer periods, but far more than we do. Quinn's words on *Rising Up and Rising Down* apply here: "...it is the maverick status of Vollmann that makes this work possible (few tenured academics would attempt it)."[29]

We need to ask if regular critical analysis works in all cases, or if our norms need to be upended. Aren't we likely to come close to what Vollmann says most will do when it comes to Kazakhstan—not pretend what he says is untrue, but treat what is presented as a tale—if we don't get angry or bothered? We are being asked to dig into our belief system and admit, as he does, that with our present attitudes we can do nothing to help Iraq's children, the citizens of Ciudad Bolívar, Elena of Russia, if we write about text. He is committed to doing something—his entire output shows the maturation of this desire to be of service—and in *Poor People* shows us that, while he has no answers, he's at least looking at the plight of people around the world, engaged with their plight, and asking if we will do the same.

"But everything that is far away and does not threaten, today," writes Solzhenitsyn, "to surge up to our doorsill, we accept—with all its groans, stifled shouts, destroyed lives, and even its millions of victims—as being on the whole quite bearable and of tolerable dimensions."[30] Will I go out and donate time or money to a soup kitchen? Will I change my habit and talk with the woman downtown who, to support herself at least partly, knits covered hangers, despite my previous irritation at her for trying to sell me those God-awful things? I don't know, yet, and the absence of an answer dismays me. Thanks to *Poor People* I am forced to ask these and other painful questions.

Conclusion

In *Rising Up and Rising Down*, Vollmann put forward the Moral Calculus, a culmination of his examination of violence and its properties, and the right to defend oneself or another, which he states has its faults. This work may very well be viewed as a provisional answer to a litany of questions posed by Solzhenitsyn:

But who will reconcile these scales of values and how? Who is going to give mankind a single system of evaluation for evil deeds and for good ones, for unbearable things and for tolerable ones—as we differentiate them today? Who will elucidate for mankind what really is burdensome and unbearable and what merely chafes the skin due to its proximity? Who will direct man's anger toward that which is more fearsome rather than toward that which is closer at hand? Who could convey this understanding across the barriers of his own human experience? Who could impress upon a sluggish and obstinate human being someone else's far off sorrows or joys, who could give him an insight into magnitudes of events and into delusions which he has never himself experienced? Propaganda, coercion, and scientific proof are all equally powerless here. But fortunately there does exist a means to this end in the world! It is art. It is literature.[31]

The Moral Calculus is a brave attempt, through literature, at distilling nothing less than world history into categories of "principles of conduct." With *Poor People*, Vollmann challenges readers to become involved with the world he describes (or, more accurately, come up with their own description that's also broad and deep, and which plumbs social conditions), as well as the book itself. This makes *Poor People*, like *Rising Up and Rising Down*, qualitatively different from what has come before. To return to a quotation at the top of this article: "I honestly believe that *Fathers and Crows* is my best work so far, and that it will eventually be recognized as such." That is one prophecy that can't come true now, or at least must be qualified to exclude Vollmann's non-fiction.

The title of this paper contains part of a quotation from Solzhenitsyn's Nobel lecture. Here is a fuller excerpt: "[Art] is like that small mirror of legend: you look into it but instead of yourself you glimpse for a moment the Inaccessible, a realm forever beyond reach. And your soul begins to ache..."[32] We can look at *Expelled from Eden* as an expression of Vollmann's outsider status—expelled from childhood (Eden) by the death of his sister—and *Poor People* as an expression of interested under-standing of and sympathy about the poor, who never knew and will not ever reach Eden, that mythical realm of prosperity, safety, and ease. It's inaccessible to everyone, even the rich.

(*Expelled from Eden: A William T. Vollmann Reader*. Eds. Larry McCaffery and Michael Hemmingson. New York: Thunder's Mouth Press, 2004; *Poor People*. New York: Ecco, 2007; also referred to: *Rising Up and Rising Down: Some Thoughts on Violence, Freedom and Urgent Means* and *Riding Toward Everywhere*)

*

The Solzhenitsyn Reader: New and Essential Writings
1947–2005, by Aleksandr Solzhenitsyn. Eds. Edward E.
Ericson, Jr., and Daniel F. Mahoney (trans. Ignat and Stephan
Solzhenitsyn, Alexis Klimoff, Harry Willetts, and Michael
Nicholson, among others)
BC, December 2007

*Over Christmastime in the early 1980s I started reading Aleksandr
Solzhenitsyn, specifically the first book of* The Gulag Archipelago,
*while working in a radio station. If you think that's a bit pretentious or
attention-getting, you may be right; I was in good company, though, as
the dee-jay in the next room, looking after another station, read* Mein
Kampf.

In the early 1990s, when a conversation with Russian émigrés
turned to their country's literature, they would invariably declare
little interest in two writers: Dostoevsky and Solzhenitsyn. The
former they said dwelt too much on the soul, while the latter was
an adherent of the Orthodox Church who chided countrymen for
not reforming their homeland. In *Pushkin's Children* (2003),
Tatyana Tolstaya relates that Russians abroad tell a joke, that
"...the Solzhenitsyn in Vermont is not the 'real' one, that there
has been a switch, that the KGB sent a double and the 'real'
Solzhenitsyn rotted somewhere in the Gulag."[33]

In late August 1989 the *New York Times* reported the following:

Conservative Russian nationalists consider Mr. Solzhenitsyn a
martyr to the worldly ideology of Marx and Lenin, and an
icon of ancient Russian values of faith and discipline they now
see threatened by the Westernizing influence of Mr.
Gorbachev.

"It would be in the spirit of glasnost to discuss
Solzhenitsyn," said the novelist Andrei Bitov. "But the very
second we begin, we become hostile camps—liberals and

chauvinists, Russophiles and Russophobes."

That same animosity is present in Zinovy Zinik's 3,300-word one-sided rehash of Aleksandr Solzhenitsyn's life presented in the *TLS* in March 2007, occasioned by the publication of this *Reader* (to which he devoted approximately 300 words). He starts badly. The very first sentence, about *The Gulag Archipelago*, reads: "Not many writers could claim that they had introduced new words into the vocabulary of other nations..." Thus, this towering work that lays history bare, that addresses what could only be whispered about throughout the entire Soviet Union for decades, and that exploded naïve beliefs held by the Left everywhere concerning the USSR's Communism, is reduced to something that is barely more than a novelty product.

Solzhenitsyn's reputation started sinking in the West with his 8 June 1978 Harvard Commencement Address, "A World Split Apart," which Eric Ericson and Daniel Mahoney state in the *Reader* "was the most controversial and commented upon public speech" he gave outside his homeland. In that speech Solzhenitsyn declared:

A decline in courage may be the most striking feature that an outside observer notices in the West today... Such a decline in courage is particularly noticeable among the ruling and intellectual elites, causing an impression of a loss of courage by the entire society... Must one point out that from ancient times a decline in courage has been considered the first symptom of the end?

He continued, to the dismay of the cream of America's student population, "But should I be asked, instead, whether I would propose the West, such as it is today, as a model to my country, I would frankly have to answer negatively."

Pierre Hart wrote in *The Cambridge Companion to Modern*

Russian Culture (1999): "the critical tone of his analysis of Western culture left many in his audience nonplused..." Solzhenitsyn's adoption by America's Right (in publications like the *National Review* and by those around Ronald Reagan) determined, to some extent, the reception of his later writings.

In a polarised environment shaped by commentaries like those of Tolstaya and Zinik, and the *National Review*, it's worth asking what purpose this *Reader* is meant to serve, and why it is coming out now. Of course since the author will be turning 90 in 2008, it's certainly an appropriate way to celebrate his life's work. However, additional reasons given by the editors are entirely practical: they felt there needed to be one book that would represent every genre Solzhenitsyn wrote in, and that would place his thought in context, especially the impetus for his later controversial works, *Russia in Collapse* (1998) and *Two Hundred Years Together* (vol. 1, 2001; vol. 2, 2002). These books address Russia's current state and the country's "Jewish question" respectively. Ericson and Mahoney know that it is an uphill battle to get Western readers, outside certain academic circles, to read Solzhenitsyn with an open mind; his religious, cultural, and political beliefs tend to stigmatize him. Still, it is odd that some writers from Russia, who may have benefitted from Solzhenitsyn's daring, have essentially exiled him in their minds because he believes that the conservative Orthodox Church is a means to Russia's salvation, and because he wishes to revitalize the Russian language, which he thinks has been adulterated or impoverished under Lenin, Stalin, their successors and acolytes. What ought to be remembered by his critics—though there is certainly much to argue with in Solzhenitsyn's thought—is that they, like him, benefit from freedom of speech.

In a lecture included in the *Reader*, Solzhenitsyn speaks very clearly about the importance of religion, and says that the "main cause of the ruinous Revolution that swallowed up some sixty million of our people" is that men forgot God. "For tens of millions of laymen access to the Church was blocked, and they were forbidden to bring up their children in the faith: Religious parents were wrenched from their children and thrown into prison, while the children were turned from the faith by threats and lies." Yet it should be pointed out that totalitarianism inevitably results in mass murder, and that millions of people can be killed with or without the invocation of religious belief. As for the many arguments made to rescue or preserve a language—now reminiscent of Orwell's writing on English, and the French Academy's pronouncements—they are sometimes overly nostalgic and melodramatic. From *Russia in Collapse* comes this diagnosis:

Our national consciousness has fallen into lethargy. We barely live, wandering from a past bereft of memory toward the menacing specter of our very disappearance.

We are a people comatose.

While insistent nationalisms grow more abundant in the world, the coma of our national consciousness drains even our lifeblood, our instinct of self-preservation.

I fear that, after all the bitter things we have lived through and are living through now, a weakening, a decline, a fall is the fortune that awaits the Russian people...

Even if we survive physically, will we keep our Russianness, the whole of our faith, our soul, our character— our place in the worldwide firmament of cultures? Can we persevere with our spirit intact, speaking our language, conscious of our historical traditions?

For Solzhenitsyn, retrieval of the Russian language is essential to his country's reformation. However, it's legitimate for anyone reading him to worry that such thinking could produce nation- alism of the most unpleasant kind, despite Solzhenitsyn's desire for only "a clean, loving, constructive Russian patriotism and not of a radical nationalist bent ('only our type!' or 'only our faith!'); not of the elevation of one's nationality above our higher spiritual plank, above our humble stance before Heaven."

The *Reader* comes along at a good time, reminding us of Russia's violent, chaotic history, of a past that is not past but which endures and is actively shaping its ongoing struggles, while showing us an engaged and committed mind and spirit at work. It is an excellent book, comprehensive and reasonably priced, and it includes extracts from Solzhenitsyn's verse, short stories, novels, non-fiction, and speeches. Some of the contents have never before been accessible to those who don't speak Russian. Since the oeuvre is enormous in size, the editors have had to make hard choices. They have been helped by a host of translators, including Solzhenitsyn's sons. Arranged chronologically, starting with early verse, the selections can surprise one with their contemporary feel. The poem "Prisoner's Right" (1951) contains the lines: "Our right is but one: / To be rancorless sons / Of our luckless and sad Russian land." The acclaimed short story, "Matryona's Home", is a devastating and subtle depiction of peasant life in the Soviet Union of the late 1950s, while "No Matter What" effectively bridges the Second World War in Russia and life in post-Soviet Union present.

The Oak and the Calf is an autobiographical work that recounts how Solzhenitsyn emerged as a writer, and the strategies he employed to manoeuvre around the hostile Writers' Union and the government. The next section contains extracts from *The First Circle* (1968) and *Cancer Ward* (1968). The complete version of *The First Circle* was translated into English in 2005, and some chapters appear here for the first time. Next comes *The Gulag Archipelago*, "one of the most important books of the twentieth century." Here, as elsewhere, the editors' head notes situate the work and its author in aesthetic and political contexts, allowing one to trace Solzhenitsyn's maturation as an artist and spokesman for political change. Part of the astonishment one feels on reading this work comes from the recognition that it is principally one man who, working in strictest secrecy, was able to set down this impassioned account of the penal camps.

What comes next are segments from the four novels comprising the 6000-page quartet *The Red Wheel*: the novels themselves are *August 1914* (1989, full version), *November 1916* (1999), *March 1917* (1989), and *April 1917* (1991). Neither the third nor fourth volume is scheduled to appear in English, unfortunately, so the extracts are particularly welcome. The first two works capture a history that might never have reached popular awareness without Solzhenitsyn. The editors tell us that according to some critics "the events that Solzhenitsyn describes are far removed from the concerns of contemporary Western readers, too alien or 'Russian,' their comprehension too demanding to be of real interest to the harried contemporary reader." Those who are interested in gaining a full appreciation for how the Russian Revolution gained momentum will appreciate the scope of *The Red Wheel*. Its powerful, assured writing showcases the refinement of the multiple perspective method used to such stunning effect in *The Gulag Archipelago*.

The *Reader* proceeds with extracts from *Russia in Collapse* and *Two Hundred Years Together*, followed by "Essays and Speeches," including the stirring and powerful, as well as arguable, Nobel and Harvard addresses. "Miniatures" closes *The Solzhenitsyn Reader*. These prose poems, a natural bookend to the verse written at the beginning of Solzhenitsyn's artistic life, are couched in a gentle, ruminative tone. One piece, titled "Growing Old," reads in part:

There is warmth in watching little children at play, seeing them gain in strength and character. There is even warmth to be drawn from the waning of your own strength compared with the past—just to think how sturdy I once used to be! You can no longer get through a whole day's work at a stretch, but how good it is to slip into the brief oblivion of sleep, and what a gift to wake once more to the clarity of your second or third morning of the day.

This twilight mode is yet another aspect of Solzhenitsyn's art and philosophy, which this commendable and worthy *Reader* presents with care and respect.

Part II: Selected Reviews

Canadian Tales

The Big Dream, by Rebecca Rosenblum
QC, 4 June 2012

Most work in the United States is an expression of contempt for the people who must perform it. Most work is humiliating, stripped of worthy skills, destructive, and tedious. Even the most sought after jobs are places of real human misery: boredom.

The despair of work, because it is a despair that all oligarchs depend on, is never seriously addressed by liberalism. Even for unions, it's off the table. If it weren't, they'd never have gotten a seat at the table in the first place. Instead, we hear: "You're lucky to have a job." In the meantime, what Karl Marx's son-in-law, Paul Lafargue, called the "dogma of work" makes its way, physically and spiritually impoverishing those who kneel before it.[1]

Curtis White posted the above while I considered Rebecca Rosenblum's story cycle, *The Big Dream*. What is wrong with those of us who spend time in dead-end jobs that scrape away our insides?

The Big Dream is set in a magazine company, Dream Inc., which has a line of publications like *Dream Car*, *Dream Condo*, and the faintly redundant *Dream Romance*. Its Ontario office is located in the city of Mississauga, just outside Toronto (nearer the airport than the "central location" employees in the opening story, "Dream Big," would prefer), at a time of economic downturn. The non-chronological arrangement of the stories allows for time to flow forward and backward, providing mild suspense or multiple sidelong perspectives on events not shown directly, while the characters in this *arbeitsroman* (a fiction title about work, and the workplace) weaken and shiver in the increasingly dire atmosphere of a company whose niche, paper-dependent products stand slender chances of thriving in a dot-com age. (That the business is failing says something about the quality of those dreams, but that goes untouched.) Some of the stories dwell on the failure of the business. "Research" begins ominously: "The Research Department at Dream Magazines has been reduced." What's left is one woman, identified with and by her department, who watches as her colleagues' cubicles are dismantled. (Though a good story, "Research" is blemished partway through when Rosenblum drops an oblique approach to corporate ways, turning promising material into a psychological study. The loss of distinctness is regrettable.) In "Dream Inc.," the penultimate story, management discuss, then avoid, a layoff session.

In this book about work, we don't often see people working. Instead, we hear complaints from employees about their cafeteria, about other employees, and about what it costs, in human terms, to work in the place of others' dreams. This is best shown in the effective "How to Keep Your Day Job," featuring a new female employee, "you," advised by an experienced, omnipotent, and anonymous colleague (or the workplace equivalent of a household god) on how to get along in a hostile environment. "Your colleagues might not like you even if you don't whine," starts one paragraph.

> If, at 4:07, a superior finds something that must be completed by the next morning, say you can't stay if you can't stay. Explain that to do overtime, you'll need some notice because you have lots of responsibilities (use the words *overtime* and *responsibilities*—they are more imposing than *work late* and *stuff to do*). If your superior doesn't respond, explain about the show, the workshop, or your partner's desire to have you home by six.

Then look sad. Then go sit down and do the work.

There is no relief at home. "Do not moan to your partner that you are imprisoned away from your real life, squashed and stifled, unmotivated and under-appreciated. He'll only tell you to move the canvases out of the living room if you're not going to work on them. Your partner hates whiners." Rosenblum underlines the similarities between an office job and one's love life: both require acquiescence, muteness, and a trashing of self-worth. Tenderness has no place in a relationship or on the job. "Complimentary Yoga" goes to the other extreme. A poor employee becomes infatuated, or something creepily close, with his female supervisor. He eventually confronts her physically in what can only be perceived as a threatening way, except to him. "She's afraid, that's what she is, the stupid cunt, afraid of *him*, when he loves her and buys her gifts. He puts his arms around her, presses her wet face into the front of his shirt to dry her tears. He hugs her so tight."

In this workplace filled with creeps, workaholics, and the insecure, it's refreshing to have a girlfriend of an employee emphasize what shouldn't be forgotten: "'Overtime is optional.' She waved the knife absently. 'Real life is not optional.'" Her boyfriend mentally responds: "It was sweet of her to think this. Sweet and delusional." Here is the crux of the situation: when one's private life becomes secondary to work, society is in a rotten state. "He was wasting a perfectly good girlfriend," admits the man in "Dream Big," who nevertheless persists in White's "despair of work."

The prose in these 13 stories (plus some emails) contains rueful truths ("Her mother would have watched Yaël's whole life on cable, in real time, had there been such a station," from "The Anonymous Party"), swift portraits (in "Sweet" a child is described as a "fat angry grandson"), and depths of feeling ("How to Keep Your Day Job," and "The Weather I'm Under," where a young woman shows an older woman "respect" by removing both her earbuds while they speak). Almost-casual lines, never pitched at a sitcom level, stand out in a prose that, unfortunately, does not demand much from the reader. *The Big Dream* pales in comparison to the recent story collections *Night Soul and Other Stories* (Joseph McElroy) and *Widow* (Michelle Latiolais). McElroy's book stands out for ingeniously making multiple levels of event and narrative occur almost at the same time, matching them to tremendous gusts of feeling, while Latiolais's work is distinguished by its anger and sadness tied to a brave exploration of what the bereaved feel. Except occasionally, Rosenblum doesn't venture far enough with her prose.

Similarly, the overall temperature of the collection is moderate, and the result is a missed opportunity to present readers with an incisive, damning, and thorough criticism of the work-life situation Rosenblum has re-created. Perhaps this is a matter of temperament, and she'll write something heated soon. Rosenblum is not subversive and challenging, and she could look, for recent exemplars of those qualities, to Alexandra Chasin's and A.D. Jameson's short stories, which don't much care if the reader understands them right off. They accept that they're not for everyone. They challenge on the level of the sentence, in their ideas, in their aggressiveness, and they don't ask to be liked. Rosenblum's geniality, while pleasant, can only go so far.

As large as the aesthetic question is the awareness, as White indicates above, of the humiliating nature of most work, and a pursuit of the motivation behind those who choose to work in a place that uses them harshly. On 29 June 2011 Rosenblum stated at the blog site 49th Shelf:

> I wanted to write the stories in *The Big Dream* because I find people in their working lives so worth thinking and writing about. I often think that literature is missing that—missing that emotional and intellectual life continues at work, and that

boring work does not necessarily equal a boring person. Actually, not only literature but lots of real people miss that jobs are a part of life, not a distraction from it.[2]

But what *kind* of life is it? Inertia and sadness reside on almost every page of this collection, highlighted by flashes of humor, and we close the book no wiser as to why workers return to a hostile, unforgiving space every day. *The Big Dream* isn't interested in such a topic. For all its entertaining charms, that lack of engagement makes it less satisfying as an arbeitsroman than its individual parts.

*

Ascension, by Steven Galloway
BC, September 2003

Steven Galloway's second novel presents the misfortunes of the Magnificent Ursari Troupe, a Romany family of wirewalkers. At the age of nine, Salvo, the main character, witnesses the murder of his parents when a non-Romany mob sets his home on fire. After escaping the village he ascends a church steeple and tears out his soul. With this purposeful action he leaves behind childhood and enters the harsh world of itinerant beggars, becoming a fearful man whose strength, in a reverse of Antaeus, manifests itself primarily in the air. When Salvo reunites with his elder brother András and younger sister Etel, they travel through Europe, the United States, and Canada, gathering and shedding acquaintances, spouses, and children. The family is placed in precise historical times: the end of the First World War, Germany in 1937, the United States before and during the Second World War as circuses peak in popularity.

How their story is told is more notable than the story itself. The opening chapter shows a flaw in Galloway's execution. As Salvo walks across a wire strung between the World Trade Center's Twin Towers, 1,400 feet above pavement, there should be some dramatic tension, but this is denied as he, and the narrative, wander from the immediate circumstances into background material or thoughts on rye whisky. In the rest of the novel Salvo emphasizes that when one is on the wire only the wire exists. His departure from his own discipline is never explained in the narrative, and this undercuts the portrait of a character whose domineering personality is fundamentally fascist.

Placed before readers are detailed accounts of what each Ursari does on the wire, and while this earnest fidelity is admirable, the physical grace of an athlete does not come across in the flat verbal photographs Galloway favours. In short exchanges, too, the language is drab:

> When Salvo informed Cole Fisher-Fielding of his decision not to use a net, his reaction was mixed. The pure circus enthusiast in him loved the idea. And he knew audiences would go for it. But the F-F was known as a safe circus; no one had ever died while performing in the Extravaganza. He expressed his safety concerns to deaf ears. In the end Cole relented.

There are real concerns here, but wan verbs, stop-start sentences, and clichés prevent their emergence. Elsewhere, the big top is "packed to bursting," hot teacups are "cradled," audiences "gasp," and people are "on the verge of tears." Historically important events and potentially charged exchanges are presented in a language that is comfortably small and safe.

It might be argued that by using familiar expressions and simple sentences Galloway is placing *Ascension* on the level of folklore, fitting his literary effort in with the novel's interspersed Romany tales. Certainly the Ursari attitude toward other people and life in general matches the myth-laden and desperate world summoned by the tales the boys heard from their father.

However, it is more likely that Galloway has been hampered by a desire to stay close to his notebooks. Unlike his main character, he is earthbound, tethered to dry facts, with the result that the plot is predictable, the characters dispensable, and the prose a journalese that refuses poetry and insight, admits little humour, and never rises above the mundane. While Salvo juts a leg out or wobbles to sell his death-defying walks to the audience, regrettably there is no parallel bravado on the author's part, resulting in writing that is all net, no wire.

*

And Also Sharks, by Jessica Westhead
RT, Fall 2011

Jessica Westhead has a mouth on her—and by that I mean the deadpan narrative voice in *And Also Sharks*, though sometimes characters share that voice. Her earlier novel, *Pulpy & Midge* (Coach House Press, 2007), was set in an office; in this collection of 15 stories she returns to that environment, and explores the nuances of relationships between couples, friends, and the worries of the occasional loner.

Particular stories stand out. "Unique and Life-Changing Items" begins dryly: "The US president was in the news again, saying nice things about his wife. Pauline wished he would stop doing that because Dale never complimented her in public, or when they were alone either, and because the president and the first lady were making news all the time, it was hard not to compare the two relationships." On the next page there is this passage: "Dale was always throwing out the newspaper and the grocery flyers before Pauline had a chance to read them, so she'd started putting sticky notes on the things she wanted to read, to stop him from throwing them away. The sticky notes said, 'Please leave.'" Pauline is dissatisfied with Dale, and while she's not completely unreliable, she is also pregnant and nervous. We need to remember to pull back and regard equally both the main character and her husband as figures Westhead has put in certain situations because that quiet voice draws us like a magnet to favour one or another character.

In "Coconut," Shelley, a kleptomaniac, busily hollows herself out. "At the resort, she drank all day and danced all night and swam in the ocean, where she worried about sharks at first but as the week went on she worried less, and by the end she had no worries at all." Her descent into a life of drink and figurative darkness, her refusal to be troubled by the "sharks" (a symbol of the unconscious, seen to be a menace) and the terrible crime she commits, tell us that Shelley has chosen to stop short of becoming a full adult. She's not too far removed from Tammy and Bruce of "Todd and Belinda Rivers of 780 Strathcona," who crash a party Todd and Belinda might be at because Tammy wants to return their *People* magazine. She only knows their name and address from the label on the cover. This thin premise is all that's needed for an investigation of one couple's marriage and their obliviousness to boundaries.

Those who are offbeat or interfering fascinate Westhead as much as immature people like Tammy. The dynamics of working life feature in several stories, but are best shown in "We Are All About Wendy Now," where an office fascist named Sherry determines that everyone must help an ill employee. Other staff fall in line, but Eunice, the narrator, cares more for her cat. She resists the peer pressure to do things to make the absent Wendy's life better, while Sherry can't conceive how anyone would love an animal over a person one barely knows. Eunice quietly strikes a blow against authority.

Some stories replace the deadpan voice with an earnestness that communicates a lesson born of loss. In "Brave Things That Kids Do" two female artists are talking, and one refers to a mutual acquaintance: "And eventually when she started coming around again, all she wanted to talk about was her dead baby. And come on, if you're not going to translate that event into a narrative that people can understand, or even that people have trouble understanding but then they can at least refer to the artist's statement, then where is the value in life's sad times?" This crudeness disturbs the main character, who had a boyfriend until recently, and who has just ended a pregnancy. Her clear-eyed sensitivity is threatened by aesthetics, but she saves herself.

As one passive-aggressive character succeeds another, it's reasonable to wonder if inanition is a lifestyle choice of urban-dwelling Canadians. Josefina and Michael, of "The Healing Arts," stand out for their helpfulness and energy, but slow-moving targets are easier to hit. However, the considerable achievement of *And Also Sharks* means Jessica Westhead no longer needs to write in this vein; she has a talent that can handle larger ambitions, and the skill to write with more tonal variety. She's a writer to watch, and to enjoy.

*

Drive-by Saviours, by Chris Benjamin
ABR, July–August 2011

One of the most famous opening lines of US postmodern fiction is: "—Money...? in a voice that rustled." Chris Benjamin, born the year *J R* (1975) came out, begins *Drive-by Saviours* with the birth of one of his two main male characters, Bumi, in Rilaka, a seemingly fictional island in Indonesia. "From the beginning Bumi's eyes pierced harder than any other's, glowering while his father forced him to try football, glowing brightly at the chance to help the man count market money from mainland fish sales. By age four he'd humbled his father by becoming a faster and more accurate bookkeeper." Like JR Vansant, Bumi is an apparent innocent, and he doesn't find the "sandy paradise" of his island nearly as interesting as numbers, languages, and engineering. He invents a fishing net so that his father, Yusupu, can spend less time at sea and more time with him. "The lighter workload and greater cash flow that came [the fishermen's] way... resulted not in more play time with his father, but less," and with time to kill, the men drink more. Things become difficult for Bumi; his mother, Win; and his mentally challenged sister, Alfi, as their father changes, just as life on Rilaka does. The lesson, unlearned by Bumi, is that innovation, if not accompanied by sufficient thought about its ramifications, can lead to troubling social and domestic problems.

Further changes come in the young boy's life when Indonesia's dictator-president, Suharto, sees "a chance to get some easy money from the World Bank," as one mentor tells Bumi, by enacting a policy to better educate the population. Benjamin prioritizes the effects: "Rilaka was hard hit by this development and the new needs it created. Twenty percent of the labour force was to be siphoned away like overpriced gas, the twenty per cent that ate the least. And with Bumi's departure they would lose their top engineer, bookkeeper and translator. But all these losses were nothing compared to the departure of fifteen children aged six to eleven years." Maybe the villagers feel that way, but Benjamin underlines the economic impact. From the first pages, he establishes a narrative in which people are objects that can be moved around, disposed of, and treated as commodities. Under the auspices of enlightenment, education, like commerce, is an instrument of oppression.

A sizable part of the novel has chapters that alternate between showing Bumi as he grows up, gets married, becomes a father, and gets into serious trouble, and the adult life of Mark, a social worker in Toronto, Ontario, who is married to a model, estranged from his family, and afraid of much that life has to offer. Where Bumi is the spark, the person who creates opportunities through his precocious intelligence, Mark is the grump who states, "I was content when I was twenty-five years old." He can only fall from here. He has little connection with the clients he sees: "They gave me the Coles Notes version of all their problems and I made suggestions, like a drive-by saviour." His one talent is writing grant proposals that put the sheen of respectability on this eleemosynary activity. Though separated by thousands of miles, he and Bumi are connected by an ability and interest in finance that results in benefits primarily for others.

It doesn't spoil anything to say that Bumi winds up in Toronto and both characters meet. Well before this, the reader will have recognized from Bumi's rituals, constant washing, and other indicators, that he has OCD, though in Indonesia it appears he's practicing black magic. Mark manages, in one of his few successful interventions, to get him to a doctor so he can learn that he's not alone in his illness, and that there are medications and ways to control his thinking and behavior. Mark also realizes that his sister Michelle, who he hasn't talked to for some time, must have suffered from the same condition since they were children. He reaches out to her, and their relationship is one that Bumi and his sister can't have. We're given a sustained look at how Bumi operates under his condition but, wisely, not so much what Michelle goes through. This neat parallelism could threaten to turn the novel turn into the equivalent of those malady-of-the-moment books. After seeing an Oprah Winfrey show about OCD, Michelle realizes she's not the only one suffering from it:

> Standing on the roadside before a mile-long stretch of impatient automobiles with her stop sign held loosely in hand, Michelle wondered about all those undiagnosed geniuses in prisons, on streets or trapped in lonely nightmares throughout the world. She wondered if they had their own version of Oprah to diagnose them. She doubted it. She wondered how the world would look if they did.

This almost bland moment is immediately overturned when the "loosely held stop sign flip[s] around in her hand," allowing traffic to flow both ways at a road construction site. In the bureaucratic parlance Benjamin occasionally mimics, she's "'laid off due to insufficient funds.'" OCD is taken seriously, but he keeps his distance from sensationalism or mawkishness.

Outside of Mark's interpretation of her, Michelle is not given much depth beyond her OCD and her lesbianism, while Mark, adept at being selfish, rarely engages one's sympathies. Greater, or more natural, energy is put into Bumi and the picture of Indonesia, based on Benjamin's worldwide travels and an interest in social justice. Here, his references to perhaps Indonesia's best-known and banned writer, Pramoedya Ananta Toer (1925–2006), are nicely done, and he's careful to let his anger come out in his themes. Mark's girlfriend, Sarah, and Michelle are somewhat underdeveloped, and the policeman Robadise Paradise is a stock figure, as are others. But that strikes me as deliberate. Instead of placing characters at the forefront, Benjamin has chosen to write, like Robert Newman, a *roman à thèse* (though more subtle than that often implies) to get us to think about immigration (legal and illegal), authoritarian rules, and monetary and social policies, from a political standpoint. This is meant to clash with the omnipresent theme of commerce, as when we're reminded here and there that "cold hard cash" is what's needed to free Bumi from his obligations, and for other purposes.

Some people may prefer books with less social content. Paul West addressed this in the first volume of *Sheer Fiction* (1987) when he wrote about the "anti-style rabble" who, among other targets, dislike writing that "ventures, heaven forbid, into areas not 'traditional' to the novel, such as science, instead of the ups and downs of little people with mortgages and fireplaces that leak smoke." Chris Benjamin has chosen legitimate and important subjects for his first novel, whose ending allows limited hope for positive change. Bumi, in Rilaka, composes a letter at the end of every month. "He sits down in the moonlight and, inspired by the constant rhythm of the waves," Marks says, "writes me his latest symphony." For Bumi, commerce has been replaced by a form of peace with the world; as for Mark, who now works for Mexico, it remains an open question how he's doing.

*

Double-Blind, by Michelle Butler Hallett
BC, October 2007

"Of the many kinds of literary-fiction writers," Ben Marcus wrote in an October 2005 *Harper's* article, "it's the group called the realists who have, by far, both the most desirable and the least accurate name... Other kinds of writers either are not interested in reality (experimentalists, postmodernists, antirealists!) or must wait in line to graze the scraps of less matterful life left behind, the details deemed unworthy of literary report by their more world-concerned peers." Writing on *Shalimar the Clown* in the *New York Review of Books* in October 2005, Pankaj Mishra drags Salman Rushdie, definitely not a realist, off to a realist camp. "Rushdie seems as aware as any writer of fiction that much of his task is to create and sustain an illusion of reality through well-chosen details." I don't know that Rushdie ascribes to this, but what is clear is that Mishra thinks he should, and that every writer of fiction should be in his or her study choosing details carefully because that results in the only kind of fiction that matters.

Michelle Butler Hallett's first novel might place her in the realist camp, with its medical, psychological, and pharmacological details, its grasp of medical history and its characters' unhappiness. *Double-Blind* takes place in the United States and Canada over some decades, and traces the murky path of several individuals who abuse the helpless when they think it's necessary.

The novel shows a skill and confidence that appears only intermittently in Hallett's first book, *The shadow side of grace*, a collection of short stories and a novella. Here she has created a character whose voice is compelling, distinctive, and ugly. Dr. Josh Bozeman recalls his life's work from a hospital bed. Initially he cared about his mentally disturbed patients and had some success with them, by using a combination of drugs, hypnosis, and his own peculiar gifts. Bozeman's work and papers attracted the attention of a shadowy organization called SHIP (Society for Human Improvement and Potential) that is devoted to fighting the Cold War with every means possible. Bozeman joined out of misguided patriotism, and gradually the "moderate" doctor turned to experimenting on the minds of young people, fracturing their identity, suppressing their will, and trying to turn them into instruments of SHIP. Justifying his actions to others and himself, arguing that he was working within limits and without doing harm, he had in effect become a kind of Eichmann in a lab coat. Over the course of the narrative, which weaves in and out of time frames, various places, and altered states, Hallett dissects Bozeman's conscious and unconscious evasions with precision, and situates him in medical research institutes that are devoted to covert, illegal, and unethical testing. Much of what occurs has a blurry feel, thanks to the nature of the prose, which at times mirrors how memory works. Still, more time could have been taken with certain sections to make them a little less elliptical though still mysterious, while in some passages she could have been less tidy.

Hallett delivers engaging internal monologues. In the following instance, Boseman reveals a more admirable side of himself:

I don't know much about classical music, only that what came to us after bouncing off the atmosphere, the signal unsteady but undeniable, was beautiful… Johann Sebastian Bach's Brandenburg Concerto No. 2. The first part had this earnest mathematical reach, and out of that came a brief melody, a scrap of grace repeated once just as you asked it to be, coming again a third time, but by then already changed, matured maybe. Then it fled.

The word grace in the passage is meaningful, reminding us of the title of Hallett's first book and its particular preoccupation with that gift from God. Then we turn to Bozeman, who perceives beauty in the music, momentarily, yet long enough to realize that he wants to hear it again. He gets this chance precisely at the time he is presented with the opportunity to turn his back on SHIP and redeem his soul by becoming the doctor he had hoped to be. Yet that longed-for state of grace is to remain beyond reach. Used to breaking the wills of others, Bozeman is unable, by his own act of will, to alter his ways.

At its best, *Double-Blind* forces us to confront unpleasant scenes, which are written with economy and power. There could be a bit of Bozeman in all of us. We often engage in self-deception, and in these particular times we may be too complacent to protest against state-sanctioned brutality. Yet Hallett's particular kind of realism—good things rarely happen, few people are kind, the lives of people are invariably sordid, and corruption is normal—is objectionable because it clearly overlooks the more tender aspects of life, and relegates much of the world's artwork to the ashbin. On occasion, her characters are allowed to feel that the world is not so firmly underfoot or wrapped around them like a restraint jacket, and I hope that in her next book, Michelle Butler Hallett will indulge her poetic inclinations and will allow her characters more freedom to revel in the sides of life and pleasures of art that literary realism is disinclined to admit exist.

*

Permission, by S.D. Chrostowska
TWR, 4 April 2014

In *Permission* we read a sequence of emails from a female letter-writer who identifies herself first by the initials FW, then as F. Wren, and eventually Fearn Wren, to an unnamed male filmmaker/writer who is told in the first letter that responses and acknowledgements aren't needed: "That is to say, I want nothing in return, nothing tangible—*only permission to continue this spectral writing, so disembodied and out of place, so easily disavowed.*" In the preamble to the book, a narrator (possibly Wren, since as time goes on she mentions that these letters are a book) outlines how the letters were sent at regular intervals and speculates on what the recipient, at one point called "Dr. Nettle," would make of the one-sided correspondence: "One imagines also that initially he was too put off by their intellectual arrogance and posturing to have genuine interest in them." There would also be "increasingly cursory attention" paid to the notes.

Towards the end of the book, slightly over nine months since the first email in July 2007, Wren writes that

it would not surprise me if you once felt closer to me than you do today. Without knowing a thing about me, you might have even thought me a kindred spirit. But now—now that I have made my strangerhood explicit—I feel you do not know what to make of me anymore. And could I expect you to trust anyone under a false name—this ludicrous moniker that may or may not have roots in a fondness for ferns (!) and wrens (!), ferns *and* wrens (!)? Personally, I would not trust such a person.

Trust is given over in the choice of the recipient, however, that he may be willing to go along with Wren's conceit. It was also present in S.D. Chrostowska's writing process, as she explained in an interview with Dalkey's Cailin Neal[3]:

CN: Were there ever times when you wished your reader would break his or her silence? Were there ever times of paranoia when you were convinced that your words weren't being read or the reader disliked your notes? Or did you always have this sense of "permission" from your reader?

SD C: This was the exciting part of the experience. Any day I could be told to stop, or worse: asked about my identity. I was never sure whether or not I was being read — except maybe once. In any case, the only way the addressee could prove they understood me was by not replying. But perhaps I did not understand myself. Perhaps if they wrote something back I would have dropped the conceit and continued the book together. I'll admit that was sometimes a wish. But day to day it was crucial to be deprived of any recognition, maybe forever. This worked well. All the doubts one had concerning permissiveness, poetic license, made it into the book: what's inherently permitted to writers, or to artists generally, where should they draw the line, how do they respond should someone draw that line for them...

During an interview[4] with *3:AM*, Chrostowska expanded on what her book attempts to do:

I imagine that countless so-called postmodern novels draw attention to the limits of the novel and in that sense expand it. My book does not. *Permission* does borrow the trappings of the epistolary novel, but its aim is not to expand that genre. It's to expand the art of letter-writing.

I wasn't writing a novel.

As readers of the finished book, not participants in its construction, how we respond to the novel's purpose is our own business.

It's soon clear that there will be no easily graspable centre, no drama, nothing in the way of likeable or rounded characters, little about scenery and scant foreshadowing; on the other side of the aesthetic ledger we are given aperçus, presentations on the Holocaust, Poland's Solidarity, solitude, and death. Like emails generally, there are parts that can be skimmed, some that have to be read twice, and some whose contents at first appear trivial but, over time, grow in importance. There is a rarity to sheer physical activity, apart from a few references to walking and the senses. Often mediating with her mind what comes from her body and her heart, Wren lives in her head. In talking about illness she writes that we should "become an instrument of our disease; the way to do it is... by sowing *discord* between mind and body."

Such broad statements are typical in the emails as they introduce a theme, and then take one of three paths: into theory, complete with quotations from this or that thinker, into sweeping generalizations, or into personal material (as we keep up the façade, as readers, of believing what we're told by any writer).

At times Wren is a crank and bore (in earlier times, she would have written letters in green ink[5]), and delves into matters in a way that comes off as pretentious and overly sensitive. (One thinks of those gentlemen who, upon retirement, send a stream of letters to the editor of their small-town newspaper.) She repeats what she has read somewhere and believes to be her own thoughts, such as the connection between books and the flesh as a *"lost art,"* though by 2007–2008 most people in Wren's profession would be familiar with hyperlinked texts and ebooks.

A reader can be inclined to prefer that Wren had spent less time at the computer or conducting research in a library and more time in a park, or surfing, or giving blood. She co-opts the recipient of her opinions into her epistles: "Since I owe this

solitude to *your* fellowship (fictive, to be sure), I cannot call it—
any more than this writing—fully *mine*; I must also call it *your*
solitude—and *your* writing. And, insofar as it is not entirely
make-believe, my fellowship is anonymous and virtual; as is this
solitude, I fear." An assertive letter-writer is not an always-
wonderful read.

Then, unexpectedly, Wren sets down a thought that catches
one up in its perception or its wording, as in this passage where
she recapitulates what she felt, as an only child, about her
parents as she grew up in Poland:

> You can't expect much from a nail merchant (father) and a
> cardboard merchant (mother), and previously a wire
> merchant (father) and a textile merchant (mother). You cannot
> count on folks with a mercantile bias for a good upbringing.
> No books in our house either. But, in fairness, they neither
> joined nor signed. If I were to give their politics a name, it
> would be *isolationist nuclear-family politics*... I sensed I was
> growing up without being brought up, and that, much as this
> situation was liberating, it also impoverished me, driving me
> to seek allies in surrogate families, to room with friends
> whose home-life was more congenial, whose parents were
> more alert instead of sleepwalking through life, and I slept
> and ate better at these houses, and generally felt better—so
> the inevitable return home was a return to solitary
> confinement, driving me to distraction.

Whatever the overall accuracy of those remarks may be, surely
we have seen such children, not only belonging to the mercantile
class. In a more aphoristic vein, when Wren reflects on snow she
attributes interpretations to those she observes: "Everyone loves
the white landscape for its purity, for briefly 'erasing' all squalor,
but they are addicted to squalor, unwilling to part with it, they
wouldn't dream of going that far." And: "Each infant grave is a

yawning abyss; you are reminded by it of the absence of memory, the tenuousness of meaning."

Later letters reveal the manic depression that rises up now and then in Wren. By this time we have argued against her despondent view of the world. In one email midway through the book she begins a sentence with the words "I suspect everyone," and it's no effort to break off there and consider that she does indeed distrust the world.

We (or some readers) find we have been arguing with her broad assertions and now, suddenly, realize we have not been in a privileged position but in a state of ignorance. In a later letter Wren compares prisons and schools. "To be sure, the educational system makes *formative* claims where the prison system makes *reformative* ones, but at the very core, the educational system is carceral and the carceral system educational."

Tipping her hat to fellow Polish writer Witold Gombrowicz (1904–1969), she refers to a lax school "run by a breakaway collective... Only the most progressive could set their children loose in this menagerie, which had no library to speak of and hardly any books. At the graduation ceremony, a great bard furiously strummed his acoustic, mesmerizing us with political songs." If we consider her education and home environment, in a country that moved from the totalitarianism of her infancy to the post-Cold War liberation of her teenage years, in addition to her mental illness, we come away chastened. Pushed by her eisegetical commentary, we (or some of us) had instinctively adopted an adversarial stance towards her and the narrative.

"This work is a structure without foundations," Wren tells the recipient, speaking of the emails (complete with photographs and footnotes) that will become this book, but she could be speaking of herself. Didn't we make judgments based not on foundations but on circumstantial evidence? To repeat a phrase from a letter quoted earlier: "now that I have made my strangerhood explicit—I feel you do not know what to make of me anymore." Everything we had thought of her requires re-examination, and the narrative surprises by what it says about us.

Permission is not flawless. There are word choices that seem less apt or fresh than they could be; the figure of Anne Frank seemed overused by 1979 when Philip Roth invoked her in *The Ghost Writer*; and, typical of many experimental works, there is a lack of humour, which is like meat with no salt. While these features weaken the impact of the novel they do not undermine it. Chrostowska has Wren say: "A brute fact: even great books are bought and sold by the pound." Soon into *Permission* we become aware that this is not a novel that will be taken up by many readers. We run once again down that sharp divide between the writerly and the readerly, and into the continuing debate among publishers, readers, and the literati as to what side of this widening gulf a writer should be on.

The mention of pauper burials in the province of Quebec comes as a shock, as this is one of the very few references to Canada. Chrostowska teaches at York University, and her decision to stay in the Polish head, if you will, of Wren and remain aloof from Canadian features is to be commended (that the publisher is not Canadian says something about Canadian presses, and you can read about that here,[6] especially in the comments section), as it helps keep distant the parochialism that afflicts some of our writers and publishers, art commentators and mandarins. There is none of that navel-gazing that adver-tises, like a badge, this country's cultural insecurity, best exemplified by Canada Reads (and its participants, judges, and host, whoever they may be and in whatever year), which is little more than an effort to build a self-esteem shelf for the nation. The negatives listed above mean that *Permission* will not be a Canada Reads choice, but it is a book that speaks to more people than Wren, or perhaps even S.D. Chrostowska, might imagine, and it deserves a wide readership.

*

Chris Eaton, a Biography, by Chris Eaton
RT, Fall 2013

Canadian literary fiction is not acclaimed for its sense of fun, and I say that as a Canadian born perched on the North Atlantic. Where I come from we grew up with folktales, and there were very few novels produced by local writers. Instead, we were treated, if that's the word, to the anguish of Ernest Buckler, Sinclair Ross, Margaret Laurence, and, eventually, Margaret Atwood and Alice Munro. In my teens no one I knew reached for novels about the Dustbowl Prairies, declining fishing villages, the end of pastoral life, or the rough times going in urban and rural Ontario. A series of imaginary Edens were shown disappearing before our youthful eyes. Everything was glum.

Yet humor is quite common in Canada, but except for the grimmest kind, it seems to be looked down on in much of its fiction. Every now and then it comes out in force. *Chris Eaton, a Biography*, by author and musician Chris Eaton, is a good example of how the light touch can work better than the heavy-handed, misery-sodden tales that fill realistic novels.

In Eaton's novel there are many Chris Eatons—male and female, ill and well—and their life stories have been collated into a compendium named after its creator. The activities and histories of these name-sharers provide an opportunity for explorations of identity and the meaning behind the life we lead, and the lives we might have had. "Chris Eaton's name was actually Christophe Valentin. His mother was a mermaid and his father was a dragon," goes the introduction of a young boy born in 1756, but he hears his new name, Chris Eaton, while lying on the bed of a river. Two centuries later another Chris Eaton complains about life:

And there were so many goals inside him that he sometimes became confused, and faltered, he might have done so many things, if he'd been born somewhere else, under different circumstances, if he'd been born a girl, born sooner, born later. He would have kicked out the stars. But as soon as he became a teenager, his dreams held him back.

The vein of *what if* that's explored provides an occasional intensity to the prose and allows Eaton to invent set pieces involving voyages, elaborate hoaxes, a sinister orphanage, the shaving away of nationality and ethnicity when circumstances demand it, and, in one particular case, time travel that also necessitates an underground life for the wife and son of Faramundo Costa. Also present are a not-entirely-undeserved paranoia and obsessions with disparate facts that might yet predict calamitous events, and those features, together with the whirl of activity and the interconnections between characters, bring Thomas Pynchon's work to mind (as does the fact that Eaton is the author of a short-story collection titled *Letters to Thomas Pynchon* [ECW Press, 2010].) Much of what is presented as history sounds like it could be true—the remarks on music sound especially plausible due to Eaton's other career—but the invention here, also involving real figures, is at times quite convincing.

"But as soon as he became a teenager, his dreams held him back." Perhaps that line sums up the source of the desire to explore Eaton's chimerical lives, or potential lives, in the Oulipian sense (a musician named "Ramon Quinolt" tips a hat in that direction), the lives we might conceive of happening in a multiverse or learn about on the Internet. Late in the book a character starts "thinking of her life not in the straight line of biographies, but passing in quantum leaps, so that the various stories of her existence were not linked by logic at all, but sat alone like cutlery in a drawer, ready to nourish or cut her, linked only by her own imagination." For the characters, their existence is confusing, riddled with accidents, bad turns, and, despite the light touch mentioned above, sudden and drawn-out death. Water is a particular hazard.

The book would not be impressive if the prose didn't work on the level of language, and Eaton's sentences stand out for their sharpness. One woman, regarded with affection, has "an extended neck that lolled like a dying vulture. Her eyes drooped adorably like turkey wattles." The "parasitic hospitality industry" is in "the business of competitive pampering"; someone's handwriting is "more like letters dying of some debilitating disease;" one Chris Eaton's job is safe as "no one was likely to fire the company cripple." Even the State of Maine is attacked: "In a future without oil... rather than maintaining all those aging fishermen through social assistance and trade incentives, depleting one fish stock after another after another, it made more sense to move all of them to high-rise living in Boston." Cultural references are apt: music, movies, and detritus like Pong and laser discs are not simply period details, but integrated into the narrative.

Despite the fact that much of the action takes place in the US, in *Chris Eaton, a Biography*, the eponymous author has set out to investigate what makes Canadians distinct. While the book contains a few sluggish passages, the greater portion of it is highly entertaining and inventive, shining a much-needed light on the lighthearted North.

Realism and Suffering

The Parson's Widow, by Marja-Liisa Vartio (trans. by Aili
Flint and Austin Flint)
ABR, November–December 2008

This is the first English-language appearance of what is
considered Marja-Liisa Vartio's finest novel, which originally
appeared in Finnish in 1969. Though I can't speak to the quality
of the translation, I can say that the English reads smoothly,
never blandly. Reading *The Parson's Widow* brought up echoes of
David Mamet in his prime with its use of repetition as a
rhetorical device, but this may say more about the translators
than about Vartio. She conveys with exactness the social mores of
a rural setting represented less and less frequently in Western
literature in the last century (the powerful, and odd, fiction of
T.F. Powys, who also concentrated on the harshness and the
meanness of a small community's inhabitants, is a notable
exception). Beyond the connections forward and back, then, and
across languages, Vartio added to the tradition of writing on
village life by speaking in a modern voice, and the novel has
been highly regarded since its publication.

The plot is insubstantial. Others things are more important,
and these are brought out by speech. Adele is the widow of
Birger, and therefore has a certain status in the village. She talks
to her servant, Alma, and occasionally to her son and members
of her dead husband's family who live near her home, about her
past, her perceptions, and her dead husband. Alma talks to, or is
talked at by, everyone, whether or not she wishes that. (Late in
the novel there occurs this passage: "By afternoon, Alma had
forgotten the whole thing, or at least she no longer talked about
it." At this point, a reader will doubt that that qualification will
hold true.) The recollection of the parsonage burning down
occurs at the beginning. During the fire the parson rescues his

stuffed bird collection rather than the church records, to the scandal of everyone except his wife, who is interested in the linens. We don't see this directly. Indeed, throughout there is very little direct action. When something does occur in front of our eyes, it involves Alma, and is often brutal.

Instead of presenting a sequence of physical actions, Vartio gives us character studies via a spiraling conversation about events, deluging the reader with points of view, dialogue, and variations on familiar stories. When Alma attempts to tell Holger, Adele's brother-in-law, something from her life, at Adele's request, it is aggressively appropriated by the parson's widow.

"My sister, she was the first one to see, she looked out the window, she was sitting behind the table and talking with Mother. She had dropped by for a visit home, she was already married then, but she did come by to see Mother every day. It was afternoon, like this, and home was still a home for both of us, but when that woman came…"

"Stick to the story. Go on with what happened when you saw them coming."

"Sister looks out the window…"

"You said that already. Let me tell. 'Who are these people?' says your sister. And you go to the window and say 'Who are they?' And you answer: 'Who else but them, that woman, she's coming now, and the mistress of the Rämälä farm, and third, your brother.' And you got all upset. Go on."

In this typical passage, stories get boxed within stories while illustrating the master–servant dynamic as a form of narrative colonialism. Vartio is acute about power relationships.

One of her main interests is the ambiguity behind any word, gesture, or deed. Holger is husband of Teodolinda, one of the parson's sisters, and is a lecherous man seemingly at the mercy of his wife, who keeps him in the basement. A reader largely has only his version of how he's treated to go by, and must decide if what he's saying is true. When Adele's story concerning the division of property after her husband's death is compared to those of her two sisters-in-law, the truth is impossible to locate. Alma can say one thing and mean another, or misconstrue what is said to her, which makes her an unreliable reporter. The village, a brooding and by no means uninterested or disinterested party, conjures up rumors about all of them. Adele's in-laws are scheming (or not), watchful (or concerned), and difficult about supplying her "medicine" (or else not inclined to help her with her addiction) until Alma threatens to leave Adele in their care. Then we glimpse what may be motives, but like the truth, they slip away from us with each word added to the tale. We receive enough information to arrive at multiple interpretations but not enough facts to come to a decision.

Alma's main task when she is first taken on by Adele is house-cleaning. With the passage of time she is relied on, and takes it on herself, to watch over the parson's widow (as custom has her address her employer), who is obsessed with the stuffed birds, to report to the in-laws what is happening with the family silverware, and to talk with Adele. The following gives some of the flavour of their exchanges:

"How old were you, Alma, when that painting came into the house?"

"The parson's widow knows how old I am."

"Well, soon you'll be thirty. How long is it that you've been in my house?"

Alma turned, giving her a hostile look.

"I mean, I mean I'm only asking."

"Don't you want to keep me on any longer?"

Alma always misunderstood her. How could she say it? She made another try.

"That's 'Jacob's Dream,' Alma."

Alma gave the painting an admiring glance and then went back to wiping it.

"Well, Alma, what I mean to say is that you don't know how to handle paintings... or birds. I can understand that you don't know how to handle birds but I would have thought you'd know you mustn't wash paintings."

What Vartio is able to do with apparently clear utterances, phrased in prosaic language (in this translation, despite the use of some formal speech), is achieve a certain level of characterization (without going too far in the direction of psychological exploration) primarily through speech, and at the same time prevent the reader, or make obvious to the reader, that, much like Alma and Adele, much can easily be misunderstood from the most innocuous expression.

Now, one reaction to *The Parson's Widow* could be to throw it against a wall after the first few pages. Adele's house and the village are claustrophobic, and so is the novel. It can come across as static. The "antic absurdity" the translators detect is there, though not in sufficient quantity to ameliorate the gloom and tension. The writing not only possesses exactness, but is exacting. It's possible Vartio slyly anticipated criticism of her novel when Teodolinda says this about some version of events: "In a word, all of it is nonsense, such inaccurate talk that even what was factually correct wasn't really true." To which Holger replies, "Certainly not accurate, or very badly exaggerated." "And simply nasty," his wife answers. The talk here, though it may be maddening, like Thomas Bernhard's fiction, is not nonsense. Despite the hardships, interruptions, and disappointments, each character has sufficient energy to keep talking and to go on. And they do go on. Readers who persist will find the endpoint, and the entire novel, worth it.

*

The Fountain at the Center of the World, by Robert Newman
BC, September 2004

A roman à thèse is "a novel written in the realistic mode (that is, based on an aesthetic of verisimilitude and representation), which signals itself to the reader as primarily didactic in intent, seeking to demonstrate the validity of a political, philosophical, or religious doctrine," as Susan Rubin Suleiman explains in *Authoritarian Fictions: The Ideological Novel as a Literary Genre*. In the main, Robert Newman's third novel fits this definition. *The Fountain at the Center of the World* has generated favourable press in Canada, the United Kingdom, and the United States for its critical position on the immediate and long-term implications of globalization and neoliberalism. A *New York Times* reviewer believes "it reads like what you'd get if Tom Wolfe clambered into the head of Noam Chomsky—it elegantly and angrily scorches a lot of earth..." The same audience that enjoys Jon Stewart's interpretation of politics on *The Daily Show*, and those who have been pepper-sprayed by the RCMP for not staying well away from heads of state, will welcome this sharp polemic. Among other things, it describes how campaigns are devised on the corporate and grassroots levels, how governments seem incidental to the running of a nation's affairs, and how language has been corrupted by business and interest groups.

Generally, *The Fountain at the Center of the World* contains crisp writing as well as the occasional, and not accidental, piece of evocative description:

Nuevo Leon can take the river out of *la frontera*, but can't take *la frontera* out of the river. The river remembers what it did last year: sent north and put to work in the gardens, kitchens, and semi-conductor plants of the rich. It leaned its drunken head against Friday-night urinals in pay-day bars blurry with zero-hour contract-workers, and had nothing left to send back to the family smallholding. The following spring Nahualhuas finds the river too fucked up to hide its junk-food addiction, its substance abuse, its sinister hoardings of trophy tampons and women's shoes as it crawls along the ground like an old wasp, a groggy ditch mumbling to itself and breeding jejen mosquitoes. No one blames the river if, when it does at last come back, it goes on a bender and is discovered next morning sitting mildly and peaceably in the ruined crops, a clumsy swirl of its reach describing a broad, haphazard domain while slurring the words *All mine!*

This stream of anthropomorphism, metaphor, the demotic and breathless magazine-speak (three hyphenated words in one sentence) courses throughout the novel, and the fluid nature of the prose suits the narrative as it moves from the business world to protest sessions and pictures of village life. Unfortunately, there is sometimes a lecturing tone when simple things are spelled out—as an example, what NGO stands for—and, in certain conversations on democracy and global concerns, Newman displays a tin ear: what is written comes across more like the talking points of policy analysts than conversation. Those mistakes are infrequent, but when they occur the novel is robbed of momentum and pleasure.

Drawing on his varied labour experiences and involvement with groups such as Indymedia and Earth First, Newman writes with familiarity on activist movements and the consequences of NAFTA. The action takes place in a Mexican village called Tonalacapan, in London, and for its culmination, on the streets of Seattle during the 1999 protests against the WTO meetings.

Mariano (Chano) Salgado and Evan Hatch are brothers who were separated early in life, the latter raised by an English couple. He handles public relations for corporations. Salgado's wife Marisa is killed, prior to the novel's opening, by a bullet during a demonstration, after which Salgado takes part in a shoot-out with Mexican authorities, disappears, and is presumed dead. Their one child, Daniel, is adopted by a couple who move to Costa Rica; after the mother dies the father goes to the United States, leaving Daniel to be raised by his dead wife's parents. When Salgado eventually returns to Tonalacapan no one can tell him exactly where his son has gone or with whom. Daniel knows little about his father, but decides to search for him, hoping the scarce clues he has will help. What brings Hatch to Mexico is more fatal: he is ill from a mysterious disease, which his English doctors describe as a form of leukemia, and needs blood and marrow donations. The only person he can turn to is Salgado.

Finding him may be difficult. A company called Ethylclad, which owns and operates a toxic-waste plant in Tonalacapan, Salgado's home, pumps "sixty thousand gallons of groundwater a day." Protests by a citizens' group against this pollution have done no good, and to add to the misery of the villagers, "the people of Tamaulipas state had to pay Ethylclad ninety million dollars compensation for the ten months' lost profits." Convinced by a friend to put his experience with chemicals to work for a just cause, Salgado blows up the pipeline, becoming an eco-terrorist (if such fine distinctions still exist). He flees, but his name and face are known to the police. A picture of him pops up on Hatch's laptop when he is "on a branch line somewhere in England after a flood." Hatch and Daniel arrive in Tonalacapan just after Salgado disappears for the second time.

The brothers are not flat characters but they are not entirely convincing. Narratively, too often Salgado sounds like a tract come to life. His lack of faith in a positive outcome from the Seattle demonstrations may be attributed to fatigue and the loss of both his wife and son. "He was hoping to see this Protest of the Century fail. Its failure would confirm a view of universal hopelessness." Further, he knows that "whenever things came to a head, capitalism could always coopt a movement's reformists and isolate its radicals." There is little hope for positive change.

As one reviewer correctly put it, "Newman's vast political knowledge and the desire to share it can, at times, overwhelm his characters, and detract from their humanity."

However, the observation perhaps misses Newman's intention. In the Mexico of *The Fountain at the Center of the World* characters are not products of their environment so much as they are by-products. From conception they are shaped by the local water supply, air quality, working conditions, an assortment of toxic chemicals and value-neutral nature. Hatch is ill because his mother suffered the bite of a beetle while pregnant with him. The insect transmitted chagas disease, which the mother died of after passing it on. A doctor tells Hatch: "Good nutrition, a healthy environment, fresh air have all given you—or gave you—a stronger immune system than most chagas victims." Salgado tells his brother: "The point was to get you somewhere nice where you could have a life. [The adoptive parents] wouldn't have been told [of the disease]... And it may be they hoped that in Europe you'd have the drugs to treat chagas, said Chano (knowing all the while that there were no drugs for chagas because it was a disease of the poor)."

Similarly, Salgado's life around dangerous chemicals has altered his makeup, resulting in one small, odd benefit that emerges during the Seattle demonstrations. "Alone among the fifty thousand protesters [his] long years of marination in sodium metabisulfite had rendered him immune to tear gas. Both the oleoresin-capsicum of pepper spray and the orthochloro-benzal-malononitrile of tear gas had been neutralized by the sodium metabisulfite."

Two of Salgado's friends, Oscar and Yolanda, have worked around toxic chemicals, with the result that their only child, Oscar Jr., is born with Sturge-Weber syndrome, which they do not have the money to treat. The boy's life is miserable and short. Industrial activity shapes characters in ways that are even more insidious. While Yolanda and Daniel have a long-distance conversation, she considers "all the things she will have to do without to pay for this call," among them bus fare, electricity, coffee, washing powder, and kerosene. In a way, she is made up of gas, power, and chemicals (Newman might have non-free-trade coffee in mind). There is no escape from industrialization, not even for nature itself:

Like steel rolling off a press, a smooth sheet of water is always pouring off the fountain's lowest ledge, before it joins the broad pool of the fountain. The deep round still subdues these new, tumbling, churning arrivals to the restrained mores of pond life. The sheety roll, however, shucks a last foaming hem of white water which bounces—with amazing consistency—tiny beads clear as Monterey glass. To and fro the beads are thrown in an arc. Constant pops of glass beads—hoopla—still emerge perfect and round, perfect and round, to disappear into the frothing shuck before Yolanda— much as she tries—can ever see them burst.

To describe the water fountain of Tonalacapan, one need only utilize the language of industrial processes. "The fountain had enjoyed a short burst of flourishing life after Chano and Ayo blew up Ethylclad's groundwater pipelines. So much so, in fact, that its full-bodied celebration had made everyone nervous." The fountain is an indicator of the water system's health and the nervous system of the villagers; it is has been tamed for so long that its increased activity—a flaunting of public "mores"— causes unease.

The psychological shallowness of characters who possess a surprising ability to find each other in strange cities, the transformation of a fountain from a sign of nature to a marker of industrial activity, as well as the notable omission of objects, values, and beliefs higher than the material world (the reader is told about love, but it comes across as more of a gesture on Newman's part; happiness is in the past or maybe in the dim future; religion and art have no place; communal bonds don't last), indicate that Newman's philosophical approach is deterministic. Salgado doesn't believe in the activists who purposefully visited Seattle. Any notion of progress or unified vision among them in their fight for a cleaner environment is set against the more implacable, in some cases inert, politicians, union leaders, and policy makers. Madeleine Albright, then-Secretary of State for the US, comes in for a particularly withering description. Overlooking the protests from her hotel room, breathing out hatred, she "swivels slightly on the stool to find her face's strong angle, to remind herself of her power." (That is not a casual use of the word "stool," nor is it over-emphasized.) The head of the AFL-CIO, John Sweeney, is dressed in a garment with an "elasticated hem" that visually mirrors the earlier mention of the "elasticated leather jackets" worn by Seattle's sheriffs. After hearing Sweeney's speech, Salgado "realized this was exactly the sellout he'd been expecting… It was twenty years since he'd last heard a union-boss speak and nothing had changed!" Third-World delegates to the WTO are shown to be as frustrated and powerless as Salgado. Clearly, the narrative says to readers, it is useless to think that these people can (or even want to) rescue the world from global capitalism and environmental degradation, which may be one reason why Patrick Lejtenyi in *The Montreal Mirror* considers the novel "at times a bleak read."

Within this grim story is an energetic presentation of radicalism scraping against an implacable conservative ideology. A *Salon* reviewer stated that "the anti-globalization movement" may have found its Theodore Dreiser, but that comparison is misleading. Newman is most like John Dos Passos in his middle period (the *USA* trilogy). Instead of the 'objectivity' of Dos Passos' polemical work, Newman offers a charged and slanted subjectivity that examines, and exploits, in a shameless and brash fashion, the tedium and mysteries behind the workings of the

WTO, activist movements, and globalization. *The Fountain at the Center of the World* is most alive where Newman concentrates on politics and *agit-prop*. The "fat flies in the flammable river and... chemical froth in the irrigation trenches" and the shaping of international policies fascinate him and engage his talents more than character or plot development, and his excitement and anger leap off the page. Though flawed, Newman's third novel is serious, timely, and important.

*

Fish, Soap and Bonds, by Larry Fondation
MBR, April 2009

A late chapter in this novel about homeless people set in Los Angeles, titled "Sticks," lists things they regularly encounter: baseball bats, match sticks, toothpicks, swizzle sticks. We're as familiar with them as they are, but it's less likely we're going to know intimately the batons and night sticks that appear in their lives to devastating effect.

Necessarily selective, the Los Angeles that Larry Fondation shows focuses on the ground level. Misfortune has wrecked the three main characters—Bonds and Fish, both men, and Soap, Fish's girlfriend—and thrown them from the class they once shared with us to a life spent in doorways, alleys, filthy rooms, and bars. Not a lot of time is spent on their past: it rises up like a ghost when one or the other feels compelled to tell the others what they once were like, stories that could begin, "Once upon a time..."

Fish, Soap and Bonds is written in prose that has a jazzy feel. The narrative voice sounds ragged at times, smooth at others, breathless occasionally due to events, and street-smart but not condescending (to characters or readers). Dialogue feels true to the characters, a sign of hard imaginative work, not tape-recorder fidelity. At times there are news reports and quotations from source books, as well as passages dealing with Los Angeles, that provide a sociological bird's-eye view. Grand sweeps of history (the genocide in Rwanda that Fish is deeply upset by, earthquakes which wreck communities and kill people) and miniscule details (temp jobs and rabies), frantic activity and quiet moments, are balanced in such a way that what happens next is not predictable. This parallels the chaotic, strife-ridden environment Fish, Soap and Bonds inhabit, each living an *Odyssey* life in an *Iliad* world. Their search for a home amidst the falling batons and the coldness shown them by almost everyone—only rare donors and the Hispanic community treat them with charity or respect—is filled with anticipated and unexpected dangers.

Perhaps inevitably, from a thematic point of view, Fish, Soap and Bonds go to Hollywood:

The American tourists, like the studios themselves, have long since fled Hollywood for Studio City and Burbank, protected and ensconced, for now at least, until lower labour and productions costs chase this industry, like so many others, to other lands. But who knows. It's America in the nineties. Alan Greenspan's in charge and they may succeed in driving wages down so far here in LA that they can stay. Please don't go to the Third World; just wait, and we'll bring it to you. It's 1994 in California.

The three enter the land of myths with few illusions. As Paul West wrote in the first volume of *Sheer Fiction*, "Myth is the agent of stability, fiction the agent of change." Hollywood is a myth-making land; Fondation wants his novel to be an agent of change. Fish, Soap, and Bonds drink quite a bit, and commit theft from time to time. They're not like a friend of theirs who says, "I poke my dirty needle—oh, so subtly and swiftly—only into the skin of those who give me money." They are not former inmates of mental wards who have been turned out onto the streets. A change in personal, local, and national economies has brought them down. Now they do anything to gain any job, even the most short-term, so that for a few days they can sleep in a clean bed after a shower. Little more is asked for or seen by them as within their reach.

Fondation has structured his novel so that he has a chance to show different aspects of his characters without boring us by describing the psychology behind their behavior. They aren't nice or good, nor are they cruel. They exhibit rage, they lose control, and they stand by each other. They remember what life was once like. They're like us. They look inward, and I believe that when Fondation writes those passages he's doing two things: he's saying that we should try to see the person behind the street person who approaches us and, on the stylistic level, he's rejecting the demands for more plot and drive, and less introspection, that people usually require of a short novel.

John Cowper Powys wrote, in a book titled *In Defence of Sensuality*, the following: "There ought to be in every nation a great public cenotaph to The Unknown Poor Man; for, since what we call our commercial civilisation connives at poverty, implies poverty, pays for itself with poverty, your poor man, employed or unemployed, does as much as any great industrial magnate to keep the machine going." Fondation has provided the latest literary cenotaph. It's rougher-edged than many, truly contemporary in style, with a nod to US writers from the early decades of the 20th century. This novel has made me search for his earlier books, *Angry Nights* (1994) and *Common Criminals* (2002).

*

The End: Hamburg 1943, by Hans Erich Nossack (trans. by Joel Agee)
BC, March 2005

This economical memoir about the July 1943 bombing of
Hamburg, referred to as Operation Gomorrah by the Allies, is a
work of horrifying beauty. Hans Erich Nossack displays an acute
sensitivity about how the citizens responded to the attack, yet he
never descends into vulgar sentiments or angry judgments. Joel
Agee's concise introduction tells how this work, a classic in
Germany since its publication in 1948, proved uninteresting to
English-language publishers. He had translated it partly for his
own reasons, reflecting that he was drawn back to it during the
Vietnam War because of its "windless calm," a sharp and
welcome contrast to the government language filling the airways
and papers. Agee submitted his translation but was told that,
apart from the fact that foreign fiction sells poorly in the US,
"Americans just weren't prepared to sympathize with a German
description of the suffering of Germans in World War Two."

W.G. Sebald, born in 1944, is "one of those who remained
almost untouched," as he put it in *On the Natural History of
Destruction* (2003), "by the catastrophe then unfolding in the
German Reich." He goes on to say that Germans had not
generally, or in a wide and deep enough way, incorporated the
events of the Second World War in fiction:

In spite of strenuous efforts to come to terms with the past, as
people like to put it, it seems to me that we Germans today are
a nation strikingly blind to history and lacking in tradition...
And when we turn to take a retrospective view, particularly of
the years 1930 to 1950, we are always looking and looking
away at the same time. As a result, the works produced by
German authors after the war are often marked by a half-
consciousness or false consciousness designed to consolidate

the extremely precarious position of those writers in a society that was morally almost entirely discredited. To the overwhelming majority of the writers who stayed on in Germany under the Third Reich, the redefinition of their idea of themselves after 1945 was a more urgent business than depiction of the real conditions around them.

In an article in *The New Yorker* in 2002 (part of *Destruction*), Sebald credited Nossack for being one of the few writers to discuss the effects of the Second World War with honesty and directness. It took that influential mention for *The End* to be published in English.

There are few events in this short and sorrowful work of reportage. While vacationing in a cabin just outside Hamburg, Nossack and his wife, Misi, are woken up by "the sound of eighteen hundred airplanes approaching Hamburg from the south at an unimaginable height... This sound was to last an hour and a half, and then again on three nights of the following week." Misi chooses the shelter of the cellar; Nossack witnesses what happened the first night:

Numerous flares hung in the air above Hamburg; they were popularly known as Christmas trees. Sometimes ten, sometimes just two or one, and if at some point there were none at all, you would begin to draw hope that perhaps it was over—until new ones were dropped. Many disintegrated as they sank, and it looked as if glowing drops of metal were dripping from the sky onto the cities. In the beginning, you could follow these flares until they extinguished themselves on the ground; later they vanished in a cloud of smoke that was lit red from below by the burning city.

Fleeing refugees give conflicting reports on the totality of the destruction. Writing four months after the bombardment,

Nossack reports there was "an attempt to banish the dead by means of numbers," where the toll starts at 40,000, jumps to 300,000, and eventually is estimated at between 60,000 and 100,000. "All the rules of logic were invoked to prove that it couldn't have been more. Someone had opened hostilities against the dead... But the dead did not wish to be conquered by logic." Some survivors return to Hamburg in a truck, Nossack and Misi among them:

We were like a group of tourists; the only thing missing was a megaphone and a guide's informational chatter... Where once one's gaze had hit upon the walls of houses, a silent plain now stretched to infinity. Was it a cemetery? But what sort of creatures had interred their dead there and planted chimneys on their graves? Solitary chimneys that grew from the ground like cenotaphs, like Neolithic dolmens or admonishing fingers. Did those who lay beneath inhale the ethereal blue through those chimneys? And there, among those strange shrubs, where an empty façade hung in the air like a triumphal arch, was that the resting place of one of their lords and heroes? Or were these the remains of an aqueduct such as the ancient Romans had built? Or was all this just scenery for a fantastic opera?

Sebald supplies details on the effect of the bombing, which included the creation of a firestorm that swept through Hamburg "at a speed of over a hundred and fifty kilometers an hour... The water in some of the canals was ablaze. The glass in the tram car windows melted; stocks of sugar boiled in the bakery cellars. Those who had fled from their air-raid shelters sank, with grotesque contortions, in the thick bubbles thrown up by the melting asphalt." The unauthorized photographs taken by Erich Andres, which come after Nossack's text, are affecting in their own narrative about the devastation.

Upon the return of Nossack and Misi to Hamburg, the depiction of wartime moves from the "unimaginable height" from where the bombs came to the blasted scenery, with the focus on how citizens dealt with being refugees, widows, widowers, orphans, strangers in what they had, days before, called home. Nossack worries about their apartment, which they find in ruins. "Where is the heavy old table with the lindenwood top? And the chest?... If there had been such a little something, how we would have caressed it; it would have been imbued with the essence of all the other things. And when we walked out, we left a vacuum behind." They meet others similarly robbed of family, friends, possessions, livelihoods, and also those whose homes were untouched. The relationship between the victims and those who are not is uneasy. Here Nossack's emotional receptivity to the stories of other inhabitants mingles with his own feelings, enabling him to describe how these divided people view the world. For the victims cannot look around and see what they did before. The offer of a small object, perhaps nothing more than a curio, cannot replace what they have lost, of course, but more crucially, there arises a short question wrung from their souls: what value can there be, anymore, in having such a curio? That remark would seem ungrateful, and a victim might be asked to explain what he felt, as would the giver of the token object, guiltily aware that he has not lost what the other is missing. "So it came to pass that people who lived together in the same house and ate at the same table breathed the air of completely separate worlds. They tried to reach out to each other, but their hands did not meet. Which of them, then, was blind? They spoke the same language, but what they meant by their words were entirely different realities. Which of them, then, was deaf?"

To explain the abyss people are in danger of sliding into, Nossack comes up with short "fairy tale," as he calls it. "There once was a creature that was not born of a mother. A fist struck it naked into the world, and a voice called: Fend for yourself! Then it opened its eyes and didn't know what to make of its surroundings. And it didn't dare to look back, for behind it there was nothing but fire." It is the immediate aftermath of this grisly birth that Nossack relates so clearly, with piercing insight into current conditions and a quiet dread about what the future will bring that is eerie in its restraint. "Have people made themselves lighter so as to make the heaviness more bearable? Sometimes someone will say: This is just the beginning. Someday we'll look back on this with nostalgia. There will be famines, epidemics, and whatnot. Only a quarter of us will survive. Nothing can be done about it. You have to be lucky." Luck, or a malignant power, reigns over Hamburg. "...I have not heard a single person curse the enemies or blame them for the destruction... A much deeper insight forbade us to think of an enemy who was supposed to have caused all this; for us, he, too, was at most an instrument of unknowable forces that sought to annihilate us." There can be no relief from the onslaught of this incomprehensible force—not in possessions, in family, in friends, or drawn from the past. Even music is painful. "There is something consoling in it, but it is precisely this consolation that makes us feel naked and helpless, at the mercy of a force that wants to destroy us."

Reviewing Sebald's *On the Natural History of Destruction*, the poet Charles Simic, who as a child lived through bombing in Yugoslavia during the Second World War, concluded: "So much intellect, capital, and labour go into planning of destruction, one can count on excuses being found in the future for some inadvertent slaughter. The ones who survive will again be faced with the same problem: how to speak of the unspeakable and make sense of the senseless." In these years of war, with their shock-and-awe campaigns, *The End* is an eloquent and timely work.

*

Right and Left, by Joseph Roth (trans. by Michael Hofmann)
BC, October 2004

Joseph Roth was born in 1894 to a Jewish family living in Brody, in Galicia, at that time part of the Hapsburg dominion. Before his birth his father deserted the family. This fissure in domestic life had a delayed parallel in the political world when the Austro-Hungarian Empire, a slowly crumbling institution, became an historical artefact, its death hastened by the First World War.

Roth invented several contradictory histories of his origins and early experiences, so it is unclear what role he served in the army. His homeland became more important towards the end of the 1920s when he compared the worsening situation in Germany to the suddenly brighter-looking Empire. In the preface to *The Tale of the 1002nd Night* (1939; translated in 1998) Michael Hofmann described Roth's love for the Dual Monarchy as a "memorial... spread over many sad and adoring novels..." Looking at this same event from a different perspective, Nadine Gordimer wrote that Roth's novels and novellas "are works in which are to be found the inevitability of conflicts that have arisen in what were once parts of Emperor Franz Josef's empire, following the collapse of another collective—the Soviet Eempire—in our time killing and setting in train an endless procession of the displaced homeless, desperate to cross frontiers."[7]

Roth's growing importance in European and Jewish culture has been recognized for some time—in an advertisement for Jewish Book Week celebrations in London in early March 2004, he was described as "the great elegist of the cosmopolitan, tolerant and doomed culture" of the Empire—and by now much of his work has been translated into English, eleven books published by Overlook Press alone. From roughly 1928 to his death he produced his most noteworthy titles, including the acclaimed novels *Job* (1930) and *The Radetzky March* (1932). Roth worked as a journalist in Vienna and in Berlin but, unlike many journalists, this experience did not turn his prose flat or dead. His personal history—the abandonment by his father, the mental illness of his wife, his alcoholism and exile—created and fed an anger which found its best expression in satirical writing, and also contributed to his death in Paris in 1939 at the early age of forty-five.

Returning soldiers (termed *Heimkehrer*) injured in the War and further damaged by a peace treaty viewed as shameful, beggars, cripples, drunkards, bankrupts in the recessionary Germany of the 1920s, as well as the ambitious, the venal, the fascists, and the industrialists of the Weimar Republic and Nazi Germany, parade through his fiction. The early works (1921–1928) are expressive of a mind sympathetic to socialism but not deeply committed to it or any political cause. They are considered "newspaper novels" because some were serialized and they were written quickly to comment on current events. Despite their occasional virtues, such as sharp political analysis and compact sentences skewering trends and inclinations, they are not satisfying on all levels. *Right and Left* (1929) is a cusp novel between the early and mature periods. The lead character, Paul Bernheim, is another of Roth's 'heroes' from the War, drifting through the next decade, buoyed by money, with no purpose but to accumulate more without doing much work. In a different time and place he would have found a quiet cove as a backbench politician who would speak for his constituents as seldom as did Edward Gibbon, but Germany in the 1920s did not provide this haven.

Bernheim's shallow purposes and the initial financial and moral capital helping him to act on feeble impulses stemmed from both the behavior of his middle-class Jewish parents and from a windfall, which Roth describes on the opening page:

He was a grandson of a horse-trader who had saved up a small fortune, and the son of a banker who had forgotten how to save, but on whom fortune had smiled. Paul's father, Herr Felix Bernheim, went arrogantly through life, and had many enemies, although a normal measure of foolishness would have been enough to secure him the esteem of his fellow citizens. Instead, his exceptional good fortune aroused their envy. Then one day, as though fate intended to reduce them to complete despair, it presented him with a jackpot.

Paul's manners and disposition are irrevocably decided by this event, which occurs when he is twelve. His growing arrogance is evident in the classroom: "His posture betrayed the thought constantly going through his mind: My father could buy this place." Each whim is catered to, from books to art to trips, and tutors nourish his mediocre talents. As a result, Paul is considered a genius. When he goes to Oxford to study politics and history everyone is certain a great career is in the making. "And all the girls of marriageable age told each other: 'Paul's going to Oxford!' They referred to him as Paul, as all the middle class of the town did. He was their darling. It is the fate of attractive men everywhere to have strangers refer to them by their Christian names."

Soon after arriving in England, however, the War begins, and he is enlisted in his homeland's cavalry. He is an enthusiastic soldier, happy in his uniform, until he is turned away from the cavalry and is eventually deposited in the infantry. This is a sore point for Paul, further aggravated by the fact that his sister's husband is a cavalry officer. Denied his proper place, Paul writes pacifist tracts and joins with other dissidents in their magazines and at secret meetings. A bayonet in the cheek lands him in hospital, where he is when the War ends. He insists on wearing the uniform despite the Revolution that had broken out at war's end. "In his opinion a revolutionary Fatherland was no better than a defeated one." Once-fellow soldiers beat him, and this places his name in the right-wing papers, where he is praised for his patriotism. The flirtation with rebellion is over.

During the war Paul is injured in a knife fight with a Cossack named Nikita Bezborodko. One consequence of this is that he is forever cowardly, and his nerves, which were never strong, will not allow him to be decisive or meet opposition with determination. Bezborodko never re-appears, but he remains a psychological nemesis. With the introduction into the narrative of Nikolai Brandeis, half-Jewish, born into a German settlement in Ukraine, a black marketeer whose success and role in Germany increase each year, the reader is presented with what Paul could never be, despite his weak efforts: a re-made man. "'I'm ten people! I was a teacher, student, farmer, Tsarist, murderer and traitor... Because today's Nikolai Brandeis was born just two weeks ago.'" Brandeis is implacable, but not ambitious for material success. Paul is unable to counter his fear of the man or his influence. Banker's son, soldier, rebel, false patriot, Paul firmly belongs to the conservative world of banking. Yet in poverty-stricken Germany he, like others, is attracted to the underworld, which Brandeis began in but rose from, thanks to gambling and the sale of cloth, to the disgust of the established plutocracy whose money comes out of chemicals and armaments.

This moving from right to left and back again has its parallel in the less-developed story of Theodor, Paul's younger brother, a fascist given a job on a democratic paper Brandeis owns. Germany's political turmoil is partially described through this underdeveloped character who represents the rampant frustration and desperation felt by almost all the citizenry, where beliefs and loyalties are shed or assumed in order to survive in a sinking economy.

In 1922, Roth's fellow Austro-Hungarian, Robert Musil—who was scathing about the Empire, especially in his unfinished and unfinishable novel *The Man Without Qualities*—considered that the condition of Germany was not solely a result of the

War and its aftermath, but also sprang from the character of its inhabitants:

> For the past ten years we have doubtless been making world history in the most strident fashion, but without actually being able to see it. We haven't really changed much—a little presumptuous before, a little hung over afterwards. First we were bustling good citizens, then we became murderers, killers, thieves, arsonists, and the like, but without really experiencing anything. Is there any doubt about this? Life goes on just as before, only a little more feebly, with a touch of the invalid's caution; the effect of the war was more festive than Dionysian, and the revolution has taken its seat in parliament. So we have been many things, but we haven't changed; we have seen a lot and perceived nothing.[8]

As mentioned, *Right and Left* (1929) is a transitional work. Gordimer says it was "written with bared teeth, sparing no one." This is true, except that the teeth are not set into a firm enough jaw. The characterizations of Brandeis and Theodor are somewhat sketchy, with more told than shown, and Brandeis' rise is difficult to believe. Occasional patches read as if Roth, in his fury to place on paper what most bothered him, didn't care to integrate his material sufficiently. Of the three parts, this is most evident in section two. But there is no denying the ability of Roth to express his anger when scenes are carefully set up, as in this instance from the first section, where Paul and an acquaintance are having dinner while Paul considers a business move:

> Everything here confirmed his hopes. The conscientiousness of the waiter and the optimistic gleam of the lamps, the diners plying knife and fork, the healthy complexion of the ladies, even the cripples begging outside the door, and the freezing policeman who shooed them away, and who seemed not like

an official of the state, but an employee of the diners... The cigarette girl offered herself along with a packet of Amenophis cork filters, and it was wonderful to know one had enough money for 365 nights of cigarette girl. Soon he would have enough money for years of the wives of dye manufacturers. There they sat, the poison-gas moguls, and one was almost their equal. Did they have an inkling of the fact that, compared to them, one was a pauper? No! They had not! Nor was one a pauper. One was simply on the way up, not yet arrived.

Contempt leaps off the page. In the end, Paul marries the daughter of a chemicals magnate, thanks in part to Brandeis, and his fortune is assured. He can now sit with the giants of industry.

Elie Wiesel discerned a prophetic streak in Roth. "Fiction contains an element of prophecy. Joseph Roth foresaw the total and totalitarian catastrophe that occurred after he died."[9] Roth's growing affection for the Austro-Hungarian Empire was set against his abiding hatred of Hitler, and in the early 1930s his style matched his nostalgic vision. *Right and Left*, despite its deficiencies, is good preparation for his more accomplished novels, and is a lasting evocation of a country between wars.

*

The Country Where No One Ever Dies, by Ornela Vorpsi, (trans. Robert Elsie and Janice Mathie-Heck)
TWR, 8 February 2011

Born in 1968 in Tirana, Albania, Ornela Vorpsi wrote *The Country Where No One Ever Dies* in Italian, and it was first published in France in 2005. In a series of stories that at times overlap, each dealing with young girls, she gives a grim picture of Albanian mores and customs; it's an open question how much of the hardness of the people predates their oppression under a Communist leadership. The first paragraph sets up the main theme: "Albania is a country where no one ever dies. Fortified by long hours at the dinner table, irrigated by *raki*, and disinfected by the hot peppers in our plump, ever-present olives, our bodies are so strong that nothing can destroy them."

While Albanians may live forever in their own country, they look to Italy as The Promised Land (the title of the last story) where their dreams of a less poor life among "diligent housewives with perfect figures" who washed laundry with "Dash detergent–to dry in the sun" might come true. That's the female view. The men are entranced mostly by the beauty of Italian "ladies on television" who are so much more delicious than "their withered and uninspiring wives." Vorpsi, in contrast to her characters, considers "Rome and Milan... too provincial to me." Paris is her home, and Albania is a "hostile country."[10]

Hostility is evident throughout. It's impossible to avoid concluding that all Albanian men are terrible (with husbands the worst), the women are treacherous, grandparents are unkind and judgmental, and the authorities are mysterious and capricious, whisking people into prisons without warning and sometimes forever. What can grow in such an environment? Only the hardiest people.

In "The Albanians Live On and On, and Never Die," which opens the book, this hardiness is at the fore, drawing on the stuff of pre-Communist history, and its representation gives insight into the nationalism and desperation that would burst out in the post-Communist world. "In our beloved country, where no one ever dies, where bodies are as heavy as lead, we have an old adage, a profound saying: 'Live that I may hate you, and die that I may mourn you.'" Further: "And then sometimes I'd hear my aunt use another old saying that was popular in our country... 'Your own people [meaning blood relatives] may gobble up your flesh, but at least they'll save the bones.'"

Here we have something familiar. An Armenian acquaintance boasted that having a heart as cold as a turnip was a trait of his people, and others have viewed the condition and history of their country, nation, region, or province as especially difficult, thus giving rise to a warped pride in being made of an indestructible, unyielding matter. "Our spines are made of iron," says the narrator at the beginning of these saddening tales. Albanian exceptionalism, as suspect as every other kind, will be presented to us by young female narrators, but none undercut it too directly; they're more circumspect; this nature of a people who have little else they can safely call their own is surrounded by a kind of silence, as if there was an intake of breath. We can interpret from this breathlessness that there is not agreement on the part of the narrators, that they see the crushing of their own spirits and that of people all around them, without acquiring the same view of life. "I shut my mouth and could hardly wait to get sick again," says one, because only in that condition does one warrant a show of tenderness.

Throughout *The Country Where No One Ever Dies* there is the absence of fathers: many are in prison as political or common criminals. To be the daughter of a political prisoner is to remind those not jailed of their family's disgrace. Ormira, in "Yolk," feels pressure to be a better student than others. One day she brings some seemingly harmless postcards to school. They are, of course, "Old Italian" ones that feature a sky, a house, and in the air "winged, childlike figures with rosy cheeks and golden curls." Her teacher beats the children with a metal yardstick heated up by the classroom woodstove. Ormira returns home that day with purple, blistered legs, too afraid to tell her mother for fear of another beating "since she was so nervous now [that] everything was my fault." During the beating Ormira asks for more punishment so she won't be a "whore"—the common accusation against any attractive girl or woman—and promises to regard angels as "enemies of the Party, the Mother of Us All."

Though the teachers can be brutal, and the rarely seen State officials are feared, the most exacting tyranny occurs in the home. There is nowhere for Ormira, Elona, Christina, Ina, or any of the other girls to feel safe from predations. When hostility is all that one knows, how do you retain some decency? It's not because children are naturally innocent; they are weak, pushed by this or that force, and they ally themselves to those who may mistreat them while being fearful of those who show love.

"Albania the Sensuous" is the tale of a trip taken by a daughter, her mother, and her grandfather to a prison. The unnamed female narrator's father is there. When he hugs her, crying, she is "horrified." He doesn't look like he once did. When she looks into a bag her mother has brought back from the prison, she sees it contains "teeth, real teeth, some made of gold, hollow inside. They were what had been missing from my father's face." Her parents divorce, using allegations devised for the purpose of severing marital ties. But now the child is the reminder of the man who can't be spoken of any more:

Now too my grandmother, grandfather, and uncle all began to tell me that my hair was red like his. They made fun of me, called me "the redhead," always comparing me to my father.

I was not of their blood, they said. I would grow up like my father's sisters, a miserable, bowlegged creature like all his kind. I would become a schizophrenic like my cousin. "There's nothing you can do about it. It's in your blood."

I would end up whoring myself around, just like my father—if I wasn't a whore already—which I probably was, as they could see it written all over my lying face. My father and I would open up our own whorehouse. We would hang up a big banner on the front door:

FATHER AND DAUGHTER ASSES FOR SALE
NO REQUEST REFUSED

119

It's a cruel and reductive legacy, this combination of fear, shame, and hate that gets handed down to children with a hopeless future.

The father's teeth return in "Dream," where a narrator named Ornela (who may or may not be like the author) watches the fire in the woodstove. "A shy little tongue flickers at the grate. It looks as though it's made entirely of little pearls... Oh... now I can see what they are... they're teeth... There are teeth without a mouth in the black hole, grinning at me. I recognize them now. They're my father's teeth. Staring at me." Death, absences, misery, and nightmares haunt the narrators.

"Water" discusses a way out of such a distressing life. There's a lake amidst some woods. "They say the lake is full of whirlpools and eddies. Many unsuspecting people have drowned there, even the ones who stayed close to shore, even the ones who only went in up to their knees." Those who go there purposely include young girls avoiding the "misery, and... disgrace" usually caused by an unwanted pregnancy. The narrator says: "I think you'd have to be lovesick to drown yourself here. When an Albanian decides to put an end to his life for other, existential reasons, he usually just hangs himself at home or throws himself in front of a bus." Yet: "Few people ever consider suicide in this country. In its passionate struggle for survival, Albania has always been oblivious of the fact that salvation can also be found in death." One wonders if Vorpsi has entertained the idea of her birthplace getting rid of itself, and whether or not there would be any salvation. Needless to say, men rarely use the lake as a way to escape. But they do end up in prison quite a bit.

By the end of *The Country Where No One Ever Dies* the reader is aware that human affection is not a given, and that some countries have had their collective will and spirit damaged to such a degree that many years will have to pass before there can be significant repair. We see this expressed in many post-

Communist and post-colonial nations. Luckily for Vorpsi she got out, and the career she enjoys is one that the young narrators could not dream of achieving.

The book concludes with scenes from Italy. There "Albanians discover that they're mortal... Loneliness accumulates until it becomes a stomach ulcer... Finally, to get rid of their ulcers, they all go back to sunny Albania." The moral of their emigration is: "The Promised Land taught them they were mortal. And they never want to die." It's left to the reader to puzzle out how the badgered, maltreated, misunderstood, and frightened female narrators Ornela Vorpsi treats with such delicacy get through their lives, what they do to survive, and what kind of adults they turn into.

*

Glass, by Sam Savage
Requited, 17 February 2013

One sees a thing while one is feeling a certain way, and then later, when one has a different feeling, it can look quite otherwise. It can change right in front of your eyes, like something in a magic show. On my down days, when I absolutely have to get out of the apartment, and finally do get out of it, I feel that I am stepping out onto a different planet from the planet of my good days; even the leaves on the trees are of another color. On the bad days I don't say "hello" or "thank you" to the lady in the market, and I cannot look at her either, she seems so hateful.

Sam Savage (b. 1940) is the author of three previous books of fiction: *The Criminal Life of Effie O.* (2005; a novel in verse), *Firmin: Adventures of a Metropolitan Lowlife* (2006), and *The Cry of the Sloth* (2009). In 2013, Coffee House Press will release *Way of the Dog,* about a former painter who re-examines his life following the death of his chief friend and adversary. *Firmin* is narrated by a rat that can read; *Sloth* features an unsuccessful writer sending letters to various people; and *Glass* has an intelligent, eccentric, bitter widow named Edna, once married to a writer, Clarence Morton, tell something of her life.

Certain elements recur in Savage's books: articulate central characters who find writing important and, at times, profound; their conflict with the outside world; and the whittling away of their self-worth, relationships, and joy until what remains is the stub of who they now are and perhaps always were. On the stylistic level the sentences, even when they contain alarming statements, have a certain reserve: the phrasing is well-balanced, and looks like what we might hope to say in a philosophically articulate moment. That Savage's career includes studying philosophy isn't a surprise, and should not be interpreted as meaning his books are merely mind exercises. They are filled with warmth for his human (and otherwise) inventions and regard for their unsatisfactory positions in the world.

Edna is, at times, exact, especially when it comes to language. "And I ought not to have said that the doorbell rang suddenly. After all, how else *could* it ring? Unless it were outfitted with some sort of crescendoing device that would let it gradually work its way up from a tinkle." She permits little to go by in the way of language use, but Edna cannot see squarely, in a way that encourages change, obvious things about her own state. Her apartment becomes increasingly untidy, with piles of papers everywhere, dust taking over, and plants dying from lack of care. What we see of her mind is, allegedly, the pages we read, but as Edna indicates, the gaps in typing can indicate an interval of moments or days. Occasionally she recaps that time, but we still only view her partially (in more than one respect). As we read, although we see her in "a certain way... [she] can look quite otherwise," and the fluid nature of her identity is something she recognizes about herself. Despite warnings, we may find ourselves lulled into believing we know Edna through the typed pages that end up spilled on the floor and which, significantly, she carelessly gathers together, their order unimportant. If she has no interest in setting the record out neatly, we can't expect to find easily her essential nature.

Edna is an on-again, off-again typist, but we rarely hear of what she typed in the time before the document we're reading. The very act of typing, as with OCD rituals, calms her and spurs her to type more. A short conversation she had at a party is revealing. Asked if she was a writer she replied, "'No. I type.'" When she was sent to a writer's retreat her typewriter was, at first, kept from her, but when she regained it she was at a loss for words. "I could not think of anything to type at Potopotawoc. Sometimes I copied things out of magazines, I typed an entire issue of the *New Yorker*, including the ads" (an unwitting example of what we could now call uncreative writing). Further: "And when I would refuse to stop typing, after he had been calling to me for a while, Clarence would come to the bottom of the stairs and shout, 'Are you out of your mind, Edna?' It was not a question." She seeks peace and order in this activity, maybe to prevent the escape of an "exploding thought." Like her mother, Edna rips things up, and *Glass* is filled with papers and books strewn everywhere, paper balled up and thrown, as well as glasses and typewriters, and there is a telling reference to her parents' unhappy marriage when her mother states she wanted to fill her husband "full of bullets." As a child Edna often had screaming fits. The violence that comes out is in keeping with the haphazard reminiscing that carries a reader along.

In that staggered trail of memories much is made of Clarence's lack of talent, according to Edna, and, as far as she allows us to see, that of the literary world. Harsh remarks about him range from literary criticism or envy — "Even in the fullness of his power, Clarence was not an imaginative writer. When he

became wildly inventive it was usually in a dishonest way..." —
to the personal:

The deprivations of his childhood made what he wrote seem
authentic and significant, but they also made him narrow-
minded and intolerant of my life, because he thought that if
one had not suffered in a crude and obvious and really
external way, in the way he had suffered, and his family had
suffered for generations, then one had not truly suffered at all
and was just acting up or pretending.

These thoughts come to the surface because Edna has been asked
by Clarence's publisher to write a preface to a 40th-anniversary
edition of her dead husband's only successful book, *The Forest at
Night*. "I thought for a moment that I would write back and
remind [Angelina Grossman] of one or two painful things,
painful to me still, I planned to say, and I trusted also painful to
them, the people at Webster and Davis, now that they have had
time to reflect." She rips up their letter, then tapes it back
together because it "occurred to me that if I refused they might
ask Lily [the woman Clarence left Edna for] to do it, ask her out
of spite, because of the unpleasant things I said about them at the
time." For the first time in years she removes her typewriter from
a closet. She quits her job, suddenly and without explanation, but
reading between the lines a reader can assume that she has been
disturbed by the request.

Edna's typing brings past and present together, along with
murky thoughts about the future. She has removed herself from
the working world, and the roadway outside her apartment
building, "the Connector," cannot keep her tethered to others.
She begins a spiral into inanition:

I take breakfast here because the windows face east and I can
be sitting in front of them with my cup of coffee when the sun

comes up. It comes shining up over the ice cream factory, the light streams in through the big windows, and I take a first small sip... The sun comes up, the ice cream factory roars, and sometimes I imagine the roar is the sound of the rising sun, as in the Kipling poem I loved as a child, where the dawn comes up like thunder out of China across the bay.

A scant few lines after that reverie she says: "If Rudyard Kipling could see the sun come up out of the ice cream factory across the street, he would be disappointed, I am sure. There are other days when the clouds are so thick I am not certain where the sun is exactly, and on those days I have a feeling of such oppression I find it hard to see the point of going on..."

It's not the clouds alone that obscure the sunshine. The memories Edna has of her childhood and the oddities of her parents, as well as the troubled relationship with Clarence, and her own ceaseless thinking—"I think a lot. I think too much Clarence liked to say, when I objected to some of the piffle he would come out with, especially when he had knocked back a few"—bring her to the point where her resources are dwindling. Savage has created a powerful metaphor for her condition:

I don't know why I am suddenly bothered by the windows, since they have been getting dirtier for a long time now, a little dirtier each day, I imagine, molecule by molecule, for years, plus the fact that I have covered so much of them with paper. Window washers are beyond my means. I am referring to the people, of course, not the instruments, which are really just a bucket, a squeegee, and a couple of rags, as far as I can tell... I expect the windows will go on getting dirtier, while the world, the building across the street, and the sun, become blurred, vague, and less cheerful... People will look up at my windows and see a shape moving on the other side of the glass, and they will not be able to tell if it is a man or a woman.

Like the fish she neglects; like the rat she feebly cares for, and is angered at due to its noises and the gaze she imagines coming from it—like these things, Edna is captured, for us and by herself, in a small glass enclosure. No one, and nothing, looks to be able to help her as her savings dwindle, periods of dizziness occur, noise overwhelms her, and her mental state continues to be depressed.

Like the figures in *Firmin* and *Sloth*, Edna looks to be completely on her own. One of the many accomplishments in this fine novel, saved for the last pages of *Glass*, and carefully led up to, is to make a reader come close to understanding the deadening sadness of her life, and potential fate, and, finally, feel sympathy for a character whose ways can be off-putting and obscure. One wonders if Sam Savage is indicating that we live in a Godless universe, with Edna just one more creature in a glass cage, unloved and not made to last. If so, then this is a chilling picture of old age and contemporary society.

*

Widow, by Michelle Latiolais
OLM, June 2011

First, the 17 stories in *Widow*, by Michelle Latiolais, are not solely about widows. They are also not, as the title may suggest, dreary weepers or meant only for female readers. On the contrary, Latiolais' prose is so lively and her characters so perceptive and engaged that strong currents of optimism run through even the saddest of these stories. This is a work of fiction, but it seems to draw its energy and hard-earned experience from the author's own widowhood, and that provides it with heartfelt and powerful insights into the mourning process.

A recurring question in the book is the meaning of the word "widow": "In some ways, it's a word for everyone else but the person who is now a widow," Latiolais has said; it's a word that offers "definition and no definition." The word's ambiguity is often at the heart of these stories.

Halfway through the collection, for instance, are two stories that present differing visions of the state of widowhood. "Gut" is a genuinely funny piece of writing about a deeply loving and childless couple. Here, the memories of their time together buoy the surviving wife after her husband dies—the story is upbeat, warm, and comic. But in "Hoarding," which follows it, a widow living alone descends into a state of dangerous solitude:

> She now understands the Cat Woman, a staple of every neighborhood, the woman who lives alone with a dozen cats, or two dozen, the house sending up a reek that can be smelled from the sidewalk—this is a person she understands something about now, when perhaps she hadn't before.

The closeness of the couple in "Gut" contrasts sharply with the state of this widow, whose husband is dead due to "what pharmaceutical scientists knew but kept to themselves, pacing, alone, proprietary in their lifeless laboratories."

In a different vein, "Boys" is set during a bachelorette party that grows increasingly uncomfortable for another couple, testing the reactions of the man and the woman (most characters are unnamed), and imbuing their relationship, if temporarily, with "a snarly, odd tension." We are given the woman's consciousness—connected at times to the thinking of the other women present—and her reactions are a complex mix of sexual curiosity, sociological interest, and awareness of her partner's unease. Indeed, with the exception of "Gut," most stories present the intelligent, self-possessed female characters as alone, or lonely, in some fashion: sometimes they're in a relationship, but are more often not. They are in almost constant conflict, either within themselves or when their emotions and sensibilities crash into the non-grieving world.

This second conflict—of the mourner amongst non-mourners—is presented from the first (and title) story, where an articulate widow, aching for her husband, visits an obtuse gynecologist. Since her husband's death her "periods have stopped, she has lost so much weight," and "sometimes she is almost hysterical." Yet the male doctor doesn't see her as a person or even carefully read the information she provided on the medical form, preferring to focus on her sexual activity: "'Wow, two years, you haven't had sex in two years?' and he fixes her with a look, and she realizes that it is her turn to say "Wow.'" The blindness of the medical profession (another doctor doesn't apologize for a wrong diagnosis) is compounded by the heartlessness of the medical form she must fill out, which "aligns [widows] with whores and divorced women and forbids priests from marrying such defiled creatures..." When she attempts to bond with another woman who has lost her husband, friends see her and joke, "Ah, the merry widows!" This is not a story about emotion running into scientific objectivity; it's about grief and insensitivity.

Doctors, friends, and well-wishers come off poorly in *Widow*; nevertheless, they are often the only people the widows can turn to for help. Each woman in these stories has lost a cherished partner and their grief is acute. There aren't any idiotic or mean husbands here, and the dead are genuinely missed. This is not the norm of literary realism, as most contemporary fiction has tried to instill in readers the belief that joy, contentment, and abiding love don't exist. If Latiolais only emphasized these qualities, her collection might fall into sentimentality, but she has a fine eye for the cruelty that emanates from authorities and society—"the contemporary world [that] forbade lamentation." Indeed, the existence of real love sharpens the sense of cruelty, and part of the bravery of *Widow* is the way it looks, with a steady eye, at the potentially unnerving topic of what life means for those who are newly, and possibly perpetually, defined as "widowed."

Naturally, the characters react to their changed status in different ways, and inertia in the wake of loss is viewed from several angles. The lead character in "Widow" feels her doctors' incomprehension of her state. She is ill in a way that they don't perceive. "She knows she is beginning to marmorealize into that character called 'widow,' untouchable, dark, by definition unhappy, sexless." But she retains a small hope: "Her body is fighting for her, for some existence it recognizes as oxygen, water, sustenance." Generally the women endure in the Faulknerian sense, with sorrow and insight, their hearts and minds working together, though not always equally, as they struggle through practical matters while looking at the abyss they might fall into, if they haven't already.

And what of the soul? The illness spoken about above is part of the internal conflict a number of these stories explore. Does the soul play a role in the healing process? "Caduceus" features a widow contemplating her own health while listening to a recording of sacred music on the harpsichord. The music makes her imagine candles slowly being extinguished in a church "until the snuffer came down on the fifteenth candle and there was just the cool, somber enormity of the stone church and the fine, fine libidinal darkness..." There's not much spiritual consolation there in the thought of extinction, but as in "Widow," there is a call from the body, in this case the recognition of a lingering sexual appetite.

Latiolais' interest in definitions—in "Pink," multiple connotations of that word are explored inside a small museum display—combines with her interest in distinguishing between spiritual longing and religion in "Place," one of the collection's finer stories. We begin in the narthex of a church, as a 49-year-old widow mulls over that word:

Narthex is the word she keeps repeating to herself, *narthex*, but she knows this is not the right word for where the congregants sit, for where she sits now amid the empty pews and the huge speakers buzzing from the aisles, amplifying their presence and nothing more.

The narthex is the lobby of a church; to be there is to be outside the place of communion and communal gathering. It's symbolically apt for this widow of one year; she aims for spirituality, but not for religion, and this story works along that dividing line. We are in a godless space on another Saturday night where many "stark faces" similar to the widow blend into the shadows (one thinks of *shades* and the underworld) as musicians play before the service. The blonde singer, the widow thinks, offers "so bland a musical offering, it falls to the category 'female recording artist'... mild, yes, almost unbearably inoffensive..." The widow is disengaged from this house of God, who is in it and what it represents. The man who conducts the service, such as it is, is dressed in "jeans and tennies and untucked shirt"; the congregants might be listening, but they can also rush away suddenly with cell phone in hand.

The widow's thoughts stray to her creative-writing students, and back to the moment to describe God as "an epicurean bastard picking and choosing with his silver fork" those who won't die. "She is not agnostic; she knows what she knows": she's, instead, "a radical epistemological skeptic." Why has she come to this church, or any church? The activity strikes the reader as a reflex, like the last tremors of the dying. "She hasn't come to meet others who believe as she believes, hasn't come thinking the aegis of Episcopalianism means anything at all... nor has she come to make fun of any mythology by which the human animal makes sense of pain." At the end of the story the widow leaves while the service is still going:

A woman seated several pews behind her looks up at her leaving, and the look is desperate, a look that says, Please take me with you. The woman's pale brown hair hangs straight to her shoulders and the woman seems somehow biblical, veiled, and she does think to lean down and say "Let's go, come on, let's get out of here," but she doesn't have a thing she can offer the woman that she doesn't desperately need herself, and anyway, where could they go.

For Latiolais this is a universal condition. In leaving behind the "biblical" woman, the widow is removing herself from the closest thing around to God. The absence of religious faith in "Place"—not solely caused by anger at that "epicurean bastard"—reminds me of Henry Miller's description of a street in *Tropic of Capricorn*, "emptier than the most extinct volcano, emptier than a vacuum, emptier than the word God in the mouth of an unbeliever."[11] The widow's quick physical movements as she leaves are found in some of Latiolais' other female characters. Their bodies contain the survival instinct that the soul, heart, and mind don't have: "she came to understand the body could not withstand grief every waking moment," the widow of the title story thinks, "that the body would insist on a cessation for a time of the morbidity of grieving."

In the collection's best stories, Latiolais demonstrates a scrupulous attention to the movement between states, and she delineates distress or sadness with precision and warmth. The attention she pays to details, whether they are words or deeds, propels us swiftly into the narrative. That sharp eye can be seen, for example, in "Breathe," where the routine task of ironing in preparation for a dinner party becomes an occasion for severe lessons on the flammability of fabrics and, post-meal, the relationship between nylon and cadaverine.

There are many other excellent stories in *Widow*, including "Damned Spot," about both a dog and a suicidal husband named

Paul, the name of Michelle Latiolais' dead husband. The abundant affection shown to man and beast in this closing story is a fittingly positive conclusion—earned and unforced—to a book whose contents have taken in so much loss. I've tried to single out a few of the book's themes, but I can only hint at the contents. For the intimate ways that it explores the recesses of grief with warmth, earthiness, and humor, *Widow* is the most emotionally resonant book I've read this year.

Outliers, Innovators, and Explorers

Gold, Dan Yack, Confessions of Dan Yack, by Blaise Cendrars
(trans. by Nina Rootes)
BC, January/February 2004

In *The Astonished Man* (1945), the first volume of a memoir tetralogy, Blaise Cendrars relates how in the spring of 1927 he rented a chateau named l'Escayrol in the French fishing village of La Redonne, in which to complete the Dan Yack stories. He set up his typewriter and wrote the first three lines of the last chapter, "by way of welcome and to wish myself 'good work' in this house... These were the sole, the only lines I was to write at l'Escayrol..." The poet André Gaillard visits the chateau on business occasionally and adds to the manuscript with each stay. Cendrars says those lines remain "embedded in [the] text," which was published in 1929. This is a miniature example of how Cendrars rendered his life in print. The memoirs are fabulous for what is recounted, what is left out, what is altered, and for their style. The product of a mature writer, their appearance was preceded by three decades of influential and robust poetry and fiction.

Cendrars, born Frédéric Sauser (1887–1961), does not have a wide audience today in the English-speaking world, though his advocates include Kathy Acker, John Dos Passos, and Henry Miller. Unable to neatly classify his work, academics have generally settled for calling him a sport, a term which is at once vague and exclusionary. In Europe his visibility is not in peril. Publication of his early poetry (1912–1915) in France generated attention immediately. In telegraphic lines influenced by science, travel, revolution, and advertising, Cendrars showed the modernizing, progressive impulses he witnessed in Berlin, Moscow, and New York where the present and immediate future promised new and exciting machines, inventions, skyscrapers, and attitudes. The first poems—"Easter in New York" (1912) and "The Prose of the Transsiberian" (1913), among others—were not naïve nor futurist love letters to technology, but instead balanced the excitement of fresh discoveries with an awareness that scientific progress did not automatically mean humanity's advancement. They established Cendrars as a vibrant figure whose valuable insights and literary devices had been gathered from three continents.

His social circle included fishermen, restaurateurs, filmmakers, and eccentrics. He could count as friends or acquaintances Apollinaire, Braque, Chagall, Delaunay, Jacob, Léger, Modigliani, Picabia, and Picasso. Cendrars chatted freely with anarchists whom he met in bars or on his travels, and their systems, plans, and natures were immortalized in the harrowing novel *Moravagine*. Comrades from the Foreign Legion during the First World War became close, if not always permanent, friends, and they figure prominently in the tetralogy and his last novel, *To the End of the World* (1956).

A Swiss-German who adopted France as his homeland, Cendrars joined the Legion when war broke out, and lost his right arm (his writing arm) in September 1915. Despite this devastating injury—Hemingway coldly said he and others felt "that Cendrars might well be a little less flashy about his vanished arm"—he quickly resumed writing poetry, such as "The War in the Luxembourg Garden" (1916). From then until the middle of the 1950s something appeared by him, in one language or another, almost every year, in addition to his activities as a filmmaker (with Abel Gance) and as a publisher. *Panama, or The Adventures of My Seven Uncles* (1918, written in 1913/14) earned him more acclaim as a poet, and Dos Passos, who dubbed Cendrars the Homer of the Transsiberian, translated it in 1931.

In the 1920s Cendrars lost interest in poetry. He felt fiction was the genre that could hold his ideas, and in six years five novels appeared: *Gold* (1925), *Moravagine* (1926), *Dan Yack* (1927),

Confessions of Dan Yack (1929), and *Rhum* (1930; not in English).
Rarely out-of-print, *Gold, the Marvellous History of General John Augustus Sutter* has been translated into many languages, and provided the basis for the movie *Sutter's Gold*; its screenplay was worked on by William Faulkner. The adjective "marvellous" cautions the reader to regard what is presented as a work dealing with legend, not dry facts and scholarship. Sutter is the first in a line of outsized men with an overabundance of energy, intelligence, ambition, and pride. Cendrars concisely sketches Sutter's escape from Europe, his prosperity in California, and the sudden downfall of his empire due to "the simple blow of a pickaxe." Built on agriculture, textiles, and trade, and assisted by the use of slaves, Sutter's industrious fiefdom, and the man himself, are unprepared for what the discovery of gold on his land brings with it. A chapter located at almost the halfway mark expresses the rupture of an almost Edenic life (save for the slaves and the aboriginal peoples) with economy, and is worth reprinting in total:

Reverie. Calm. Repose.
It is Peace.
No. No. No. No. No. No. No. No. No: it is GOLD!
It is gold.
The gold rush.
The world is infected with gold fever.
The great gold rush of 1848, 1849, 1850 and 1851. It will last for fifteen years.
SAN FRANCISCO!

That "no" moves the reader from contradiction to realization, from grim acceptance to panic and fear. This parable of greed charts the decline in Sutter's mental health and fortune, the death of family members, and his years in Washington spent labouring for financial recompense. Stylistically, in *Gold* sparse sentences

135

carry much weight, while repetition, along with historical facts and occasional longer descriptions, subtly merge reportage and fictional narrative. Panoramic set-pieces of travellers heading west into dangerous lands or Sutter's voyages across the Pacific showcase Cendrars' experience in the cinema. This novel is a bridge between the compressed lines of poetry he fashioned in the early 1920s and the more expansive novels to come.

After dealing with terrorism and a regicide in *Moravagine*, Cendrars created an ostensibly benevolent figure, a rich man with grand ideas. *Dan Yack* breaks into two parts and is told in the third person. Heartbroken by Hedwiga's decision to marry another man despite possibly carrying his child, Dan Yack invites three artists to join him, at his expense, for a year's retreat from civilization. The sculptor Ivan Sabakov, the musician André Lamont, and the poet Arkadie Goischman board the *Green Star*, one of Dan Yack's vessels. A globe is suspended above a floor on board, and each artist is allowed one pistol shot to decide where the four men (and Dan Yack's dog, Bari) will reside. Lamont deliberately severs the string attached to the globe; it crashes to the floor, rendering Antarctica their destination. It is March 1905. A shelter is set up, provisions are stored away, and the vessel departs. "Naturally, things did not run smoothly," begins one section laconically, and the colony soon self-destructs. When the *Green Star* returns a year later, the second part begins. Dan Yack plunges into his family's business, whaling, and over several years expands its market through modernization of the fleet and the invention of new products. At Community City, in Port Deception, he "wanted to found a kind of universal happiness..." Though successful in business, Dan Yack has never recovered from the loss of Hedwiga; his torment is intensified when he falls in love with an unattainable woman he meets towards the end of the novel. He suffers from a suicidal impulse that is barely restrained by an unconscious determination to act, to resist stasis. The whirl of events and the twists and turns of Dan Yack's mind are reflected in the hectic, fragmented utterances found throughout the novel. Here, the technique of short sentences, familiar from *Gold*, is adjusted to contain a lyricism that seeks to capture natural beauty and events, yet Cendrars also shows that impressions come too quickly for words to convey the experience:

An iceberg turns upside-down and disintegrates. In its fall, it brings down rags of tattered mist.

A dome of blue sky, then a luminous rift that descends right down to the level of the seething water.

A ray of sunlight is sprinkled over the mountains of floating ice, which break up and distil its light.

Everywhere, dazzling light. The rainbow is knotted into a whirlwind of sapphires, emeralds, rubies; it is a constantly shaken kaleidoscope, changing, splintering, reflecting and refracting...

The mist is viscous.

The sea breaks up.

It is choppy.

Everything is rocking.

Confessions of Dan Yack is the first-person account of Dan Yack's life in a châlet above the village of Chamonix. There he mourns the death of Mireille, a young woman he loved. From January to September 1925 he records his memories into a dictaphone, narrating what life was like on Port Deception before and after the Germans took control, describing his service in the war, and how he met Mireille. Reading aloud from her notebooks, Dan Yack says: "I should have bought this machine for her. She could have spoken into it. And today I should be listening to her voice..." Though the narrative shifts from the source of his grief to apparently unrelated incidents—the war, opinions about New Zealand, a search for gold in the mountains around him—each story reveals a different aspect of this formerly powerful man. In an act of petty cruelty meant to correct an injustice or imbalance, he plots to kill two eagles whose nest is near the châlet. Since he and Mireille cannot live together (in the same way he could not live with Hedwiga and their son), the eagles have no right to live as a pair either.

Eventually Dan Yack moves on to the next phase of his life, but he is no longer as decisive. The novel's pace is slow, its tone is mournful, at times grim, and the depiction of a man who is unable to stop death or loss from visiting him connects this work, in a natural and thematically faithful way, with the last pages of *Dan Yack*.

Short quotations don't adequately convey the momentum of Cendrars' prose, whether in the cascade of short sentences or in the pile-up of clauses in one-sentence paragraphs that span pages. Nor can a review do justice to the intricate plots, the exuberant imagination, the delight in language, the intelligence and the geniality of the work, and its varieties of humour. Peter Owen deserves credit for reissuing these novels and *To the End of the World* (there are tentative plans for *The Astonished Man* to appear this spring). There will be those who find Blaise Cendrars' style too rich, but there will be others who will be carried away by his adventures, verve, and audaciousness.

*

Agapē Agape: A Novel, by William Gaddis (afterword by Joseph Tabbi); *The Rush for Second Place: Essays and Occasional Writings,* by William Gaddis (edited with notes and introduction by Joseph Tabbi)
BC, April 2003

"[W]e are all in the same line of business: that of concocting, arranging, and peddling fictions to get us safely through the night," said William Gaddis (1922–1998), comparing fiction writers and the religious. It is likely that more readers of US fiction will have heard about Gaddis' concoctions than have read them. His first novel, *The Recognitions*, came out in 1955, and critics immediately typed him as a difficult writer. In prose imbued with humour and a peculiar lyricism, there occur stimulating discussions of authenticity, forgery, painting, Christianity, and other topics. The erudition and length of this 956-page novel irritated and defeated reviewers insensitive to inventiveness. They did not read *The Recognitions* thoroughly but talked as if they had, and their hostile opinions helped insure the novel sold poorly. It gradually assumed cult status nonetheless. Don DeLillo and William Gass drew encouragement from this vital work, as did later authors like David Foster Wallace and William Vollmann.

Twenty years later Gaddis's reputation as difficult was confirmed, for those predisposed to think that way, by his second novel, *J R*. Most of the 726-page novel is in dialogue without speech tags to indicate transitions from one character to another. Choppy, broken sentences create a picture of disorder on the communicative level that matches the misshapen composition of a financial empire ruled by an 11-year-old. Gaddis placed a defiant remark about his aesthetics, aimed at inattentive readers, in the mouth of the character Jack Gibbs: "Most God damned readers rather be at the movies..." Thanks to Gass and Mary McCarthy, who recognized the quality of this exuberant, probing analysis of the financial world, *J R* won the 1976 National Book Award.

Carpenter's Gothic (1985), a work of 262 pages that respects Aristotelian unities, met with relative success, and Gaddis was no longer strictly a cult author. There is none of his plentiful humour (by turns dark, witty, slapstick, and occasionally sophomoric) in this novel that deals with, among other things, Christian fundamentalism, the US grabbing another country's resources, and looming Armageddon. Gaddis's outlook over the course of the three novels had darkened from satire through meliorism to pessimism.

His fourth and last novel was the 586-page *A Frolic of His Own*. Comprising a traditional narrative, legal opinions, court transcriptions, and excerpts from a play Gaddis had attempted to write, then abandoned, it won the National Book Award for 1994. Gaddis' successful explorations of the novel and its potential, his complex structures, and the use of unusual material finally gained the respect he had been denied for 40 years. Yet he was still classed as difficult, when all that's required is patience and an active participation on the part of a reader.

The Rush for Second Place collects essays, speeches, and reviews spanning 1951 to 1998. There are articles and notes on the player piano and certain essays—such as "Old Foes with New Faces," on religion; "The Rush for Second Place," on the desire to be first; his NBA acceptance speeches—that will be of general interest. A few will appeal primarily to Gaddis readers. All are headed by Joseph Tabbi's informative notes. In the introduction he states:

What blocks the literary imagination is precisely what stimu-lated Gaddis to further creativity. By setting himself challenges equal to the world's own constraints and resis-tances, he could discover what freedom and autonomy might be possible, in the here and now, for an individual life and talent.

Agapē Agape, Gaddis's most recent work, retains his uncompro-mising vision and desire to create fiction that challenges the reader. It is the 96- page single-paragraph monologue of a dying old man as he attempts to complete a history of the player piano. Like the stock market and the law, this seems an unpromising topic for fiction. Gaddis wrestled with the material in the 1960s, as shown in *The Rush for Second Place*—almost a companion volume to the novella—and in *J R* Gibbs struggles to write the book Gaddis could not. Eventually, inspired by the work of Austrian writer Thomas Bernhard, Gaddis discarded an historical approach illustrating how the technology behind the mechanical loom led to player pianos and, ultimately, to computers. He recast the research in the form of a rambling address from an unnamed man. *Agapē Agape* recapitulates many Gaddis themes: authenticity versus the counterfeit, the declining role of the artist, entropy, loss, and failure. Tabbi's afterword is of considerable help and, as with the essay collection, he is a sympathetic and discerning commentator.

The narrator of *Agapē Agape* is either in a hospital or a disorderly room in his own house. The location is vague because knowing where he is doesn't matter. What is important for Gaddis is the dislocation the reader experiences in order to enter the narrator's mind. Surrounded by books and papers the narrator frets about his work and about dispensing property:

> divide everything three ways one for each daughter and we all benefit... I spend a third of the year with each of them, get on with my work... and I'm allowed to show my generosity and they have the opportunity to show their love for me.

He considers how this will be perceived: "where they'll say I never really planned the whole property transfer to them out of love but just as a scheme to avoid taxes?" As in the novels, individuals are constrained within a system (religious, economic, legal) and actions potentially stem from a variety of motives. The narrator's situation is a crudely forged version of Lear's predicament. After quoting from one of Bernhard's books he says: "It's my opening page, he's plagiarized my work right here in front of me before I've even written it!" What is one's own and what is stolen—questions from what constitutes plagiarism to what makes us individuals—also drive *The Recognitions* and *A*

Frolic of His Own.

While managing legal affairs does concern the narrator, it comes second to organizing his player piano material. "Chance and disorder sweeping in" disrupt everything. Papers fall over, books are lost then found, a pencil appears and disappears. Physically, the narrator is deteriorating. Blood leaks from cuts to his stapled, parchment-like skin. Part flesh, part paper, part synthetic, his speech replete with quotations, allusions, and historical references, the drugged, visually impaired, and occasionally disoriented narrator is a cyborg. Unable to finish his work on paper, he expresses it to an Other. This Other is himself, the writers he arranges against each other—Flaubert, Tolstoy, Walter Benjamin, Plato—and the reader. Often it is "some monstrous, some detachable self, some dangerous demon." At other times it is benign.

It is also the only companion the narrator has. To this Other he can confide his bitterness over personal and career failures, of being a "buffoon all two dimensional some cartoon..." Anguished, he gradually focuses on how his potential, his better self, disappeared. From the opening the narrator has hinted at the seriousness of his failure to be a different man. In the last three pages he confronts this harsh realization, avoiding the digressions and hesitations that are features of the bulk of his monologue; in this tight focus, order is finally present, though only temporarily. The narrator concedes he abandoned his "ideas and opinions to suit public opinion and be part of it a, a yes a nonperson looking back at the arrogant self-made self..." The image of himself as a cartoon—a preliminary sketch of a full man—now has a fuller explanation, and is tied to some of Michelangelo's words which reverberate through the narrator's mind—"the self who can do more"; this phrase appears in every Gaddis novel. The end of *Agapē Agape* is a passionate outburst spoken into that night through which safe passage is desired:

That was Youth with its reckless exuberance when all things were possible pursued by Age where we are now, looking back at what we destroyed, what we tore away from that self who could do more, and its work that's become my enemy because that's what I can tell you about, that Youth who could do anything.

Agapē Agape is a fitting conclusion to a career shaped by artistic integrity and inventiveness. Gaddis transforms a small tutorial on the player piano into a plaintive last act, filled with jagged rhythms and darting wit. He is a superb stylist and a bracing author who has been too little read. Tabbi's notes in both books serve as a good introduction, and readers can find more at <http://www.williamgaddis.org>, an excellent website devoted to Gaddis's works.

*

The Letters of John Cowper Powys and Dorothy Richardson, ed. Janet Fouli
PR, August 2010

From the beginning of the correspondence between John Cowper Powys and Dorothy Richardson, one is aware of the definite pleasure Powys took in writing someone whose work he admired. In the first published letter we get a hint of his excitement upon suggesting they meet: "Apart from my numerous brothers & sisters... there's no one in England I want to see so much as yourself and it would be rather a sad disappointment to me if fate doesn't allow it." They would be separated for most of their friendship, first by the Atlantic, and then by the distance between Corwen and London, and would meet only a few times before the early 1950s, when Richardson ceased to write as her health declined. Yet there is a definite bond between them, and the correspondence, instigated by Powys, lasted from 1929 to 1952. When writing to others, such as Emma Goldman, Powys sometimes had to be buttoned down, but here he enjoys letting himself go, as in this characteristic passage:

> I try & *visualize* the hunched-up, truculant [*sic*], forbidding, impenetrable, pebble-stone-on-the-Chesil-Beach-like Ego into which most of us have the power of transforming ourselves when we "freeze" at the approach of an enemy ... & starting with this I go ahead with the Self & the Not-Self etc etc etc using all the clap-trap I can recall out of former broodings upon Hegel in order to force my converted ones—of the Third order of Empedocles the Second—into the worship of the Inanimate as the best substitute for 'God', & the place where the wall of the cosmos is *thinnest*, so to speak, & if you put your ear close you can hear the music the *other side*. (Ellipsis and italics in original.)

Over the course of their correspondence most of Powys' major works come out; *Wolf Solent* appeared before they met in August 1929. A portion of a letter written in September of that year by Richardson to Peggy Kirkaldy is included: "The *London Mercury* gives a long article to *Wolf Solent*, mostly in praise of it. And it seems John has written other books. Dark horse, he never mentioned them." As it turns out, in the second appendix there is a 1951 letter to the poet and editor Henry Savage in which Richardson expresses what she never mentioned to Powys—her candid opinion about his literary worth:

> [Henry Miller's] adoration of J.C.P.'s work is as mysterious to me as is J.C.P.'s of my own, endlessly reiterated in innumerable letters. For it is not reciprocal. Alan [Alan Odle, Richardson's husband] loved his work and behind him, eagerly reading, I used to hide by quoting A., my own diffi-

culty in getting through anything beyond *Wolf Solent*, bits of *Glastonbury* and *The Pleasures of Literature*, embodying his life-work as lecturer and, for me, his one solid contribution. All the rest I would exchange for Theodore's *Mr. Weston's good wine* [sic] and Llewelyn's little book on Switzerland. Miller, I feel, shares J.C.P.'s over-elaboration and reiteration.

This admission can be viewed in any number of ways. Is it a pose created for the benefit of Savage, a relative newcomer in her life? According to George Thomson, editor of *Dorothy Richardson: A Calendar of Letters* (2007), Savage began writing Richardson in or soon after 1946 "with the purpose, so he claimed, of leading her through argument to assert her outlook and beliefs." It might be argued that for years Richardson displayed tact, or diplomacy, by not letting her true feelings be known to Powys. For all Powys did to talk her up, as the letters show, in lectures and by way of trying to get her collected works published, eagerly reading her work and engaging with it, Dorothy Richardson was unable to offer anything similar in return. She could not match his respect, let alone his enthusiasm, and didn't have the courage or character to say she didn't like this or that work. In a letter to Bernice Elliott, an extract of which is reproduced by Fouli, Richardson refers to *Owen Glendower*: "Dear John Cowper still inhabits his dark Welsh valley. Things are not, I fear, too easy. He turns out potboilers with amazing rapidity." When Richardson tells Powys that "they are right who claim the *Autobiography* as one of the few immortal books of the century," what does she mean, and who is this "they"? It appears not to include her.

Not only did Powys encourage audiences to read Richardson, he wrote a book on her, news which of which brought out from Richardson the gracious comment to Elliott that she was "not quite sure whether to be jubilant or horrified." While writers often remember the negative reviews more than the positive ones, generally they do like it when someone goes out of their way to publicize their work. Perhaps, in some other letter to a third party, Richardson expresses gratitude, but the mystery as to why she would be "jubilant or horrified" about Powys' views is not dispelled.

Literary history has judged Richardson's ranking of Powys' fiction and essays rather differently. His essays are hard to find, whereas his major fictional works are in many bookstores (new and second-hand), with Faber Finds enabling readers to purchase on-demand novels early and late. However, even now there's no critical consensus about the values of his novels. There is intermittent interest in Dorothy Richardson, as found in the work of Gloria Fromm—above all, her biography of 1977 and her edition of the selected letters, *Windows on Modernism*, in 1995—and, recently, Debora Parsons' assessment of Richardson's role in Modernism's theoretical reflections and formulations: her *Theorists of the Modern Novel: James Joyce, Dorothy Richardson and Virginia Woolf* was published in 2006. Yet Fouli is close to the mark when she says that both Powys and Richardson are "now suffering an eclipse; neither writer is really in the canon of English literary studies though both are recognized as significant figures."

Richardson writes letters that are highly readable, and filled with a poetic attention to detail:

Here, spring sings aloud & gorse, gently blazing all the winter, flames high now in our midge-haunted tamarisk lane-to-the-sea. But our floods don't abate. I mop gallons from the stone floor of the kitchen, to find them replaced almost before I can turn round. A broad rivulet invades the passage & another the floor of a foolish little bedroom with a no-doubt-heavenly-in-summer outer door, flush with the soil. I cannot, for the rain-din on the roof, hear myself cook, hear, that is to say, whether the stew is just gently whispering or perilously near the boil.

The anthropomorphizing of the season, the vegetation, the "foolish" room, and the natural swerve into domestic affairs, are elements close to Powys' supplications to nature and various spirits, and his comically disastrous encounters with the fire, the stove, and anything to do with maintaining a household. When Richardson writes to give her opinion of *The Pleasures of Literature* over a five-page letter written in February 1939 she is at her critical best: attentive to Powys' work, supportive, and engaged with the text, while working out her own opinions.

However, there is a problem with *The Letters of John Cowper Powys and Dorothy Richardson*. The Introduction contains an arguable thesis that the letters "are not deliberate self-revelations for the public..., for unknown readers were not anticipated by either writer." This may seem unlikely: all writers must consider the danger that their private writings will enter the public domain (else why so many instructions to burn papers after their death?). But perhaps Fouli is right, and neither Powys nor Richardson, both of whom had to struggle to get their novels published, ever had an idea that their letters would be printed. More seriously, for any editor of correspondence involving John Cowper Powys, to write, as Fouli does, that one particular collection of letters forms a "self-portrait projecting each of them in his preoccupations and his environment, and also a mirror, showing how each of them sees the other," is to say only that at heart this volume is indistinct from other volumes of Powys letters. This actually underplays the particular interest of this volume.

Further, when we look at the editor's bold announcement that this correspondence "show[s] how each of them sees the other," and then at the letter to Savage where Richardson reveals her honest opinion about Powys' work, we see something very far from truthful showing. There is a touch of impatience behind Richardson's complaint over Powys' admiration of her novels "endlessly reiterated in innumerable letters," as if she felt put upon by a tiresome fan. Fouli provides the material to arrive at this conclusion, and it's disconcerting that she doesn't notice the contradiction in her claim. We are left to wonder what else Richardson thought about Powys and his work which went unstated to him but which she was clear about to others, or kept to herself. The editorial apparatus is of little help here.

Indeed, the Notes, which occupy the back of the book, fail to provide enough context. A few examples will illustrate this. Powys mentions a book titled *Quiet Interiors*, for which the note gives little beyond its author's name, E.B.C. Jones. It is surely worth mentioning that the book was highly praised by Katherine Mansfield. The planet Eros that he refers to goes without a note, though a Google search calls up much about it. When Powys notes that Richardson "became a Bugloss" the meaning is mysterious. This appears to be a noxious plant, but is there some other meaning it might have? Might it also be the name of a character from some literary work? Further on, a Dr. Bertrand Allinson and a medication named Yadil are referred to, but no note accompanies these references, though a Google search reveals that Allinson was an advocate of vegetarianism. French goes untranslated; when Richardson asks "Is the passing of Mary Butts a blow for you? For us it is," readers are sent, and not right away, to a note that tells of a publication by this still little-known writer. The same fate is imposed on "Shaw, Webb & Wells," where Shaw and Wells are clear from the context, but anyone not familiar with Webb will find no more about him except that his first name was Sidney, and that is to be learnt only in the Index.

From 30 March 1930 to 29 September 1932 there are only two letters from Richardson. More information on her life, in addition to the extracts from Powys' diaries, would have been useful here. There are many places where a reader would be thankful for entries identifying Peggy Kirkaldy, Henry Savage, or Bernice Elliott. It also would have been good to have more than one paragraph on Richardson's last years. In general Fouli has not taken the opportunity to fill in the biographical context, or address particular biographical issues, in adequate detail. She does, however, decipher Powys' notoriously bad handwriting and his erratic placement of words on a page, which is no small achievement, and for which she deserves appropriate commendation.

Despite reservations, *The Letters of John Cowper Powys and Dorothy Richardson* is an enjoyable collection, filled with wonderfully unpredictable thoughts, and two distinct modes of writing. It would be fitting to close with an example of each writer's style. After a meeting between Powys and Richardson, and Phyllis Plater and Alan Odle, in 1934, Powys wrote: "After being with you two I felt a glow that lifted me on a wave of foamless content with the possibilities of existence & I didn't care what I'd blurted out or what blunderings I'd committed; and I knew you'd take Phyllis just right and as she likes to be taken, as your words now prove—not as if she were [a] pilgrim swallowed by Gargantua with his lettuce, but like a a [*sic*] girl with her own thoughts as she rides on the Centaur's back!" Richardson's letters provide views into her own marriage: "For five days we've been here, drunk with release, both of us, for Alan at home is dishwasher & boot-cleaner, breakfast-getter & toast-for-tea maker, from every kind of chore; drunk also with the excitements of urban centrality, keeping us, who are flush with the roadway, with half an eye permanently slewed round to see who is passing, & both ears wide for farm-yard sounds & meadow-sounds & the occasional thundering of the omnibus down the lane." Whatever the writers' wishes or expectations, the editor, and especially Cecil Woolf, the publisher, deserve our thanks for making these letters available. Though the readership may be wider than the letter-writers intended, it is likely to find much to appreciate and admire.

*

The Abyss of Human Illusion, by Gilbert Sorrentino
LR, Spring 2010

There have been a few authors whose work has inspired me to think in new ways about writing. This is familiar to most readers. Also familiar is the sensation that hardens over time into a conviction—perhaps by dint of not wanting to be taken over by a book (i.e. by another's consciousness)—that this can't happen (*shan't* happen is an older way of putting it) as we get older. We build ourselves into sophisticated readers less and less open to ravishing by this or that poem, novel, or play. An editorial will spark a letter, a government policy initiate a petition, but a sonnet? Oh, we'll be stirred for a few minutes, but then we'll calm down.

By inspiration I'm thinking of kinship, of writers who formed a family of mentors. It wasn't until university that I started reading what you'd call literature. The curriculum hardly compared to those I stumbled upon. Philip José Farmer's "biography" of Doc Savage contained quotations from Henry Miller's *Tropic of Cancer*, a title that stuck in my head. Months later I came across a tattered copy for under a dollar, read it, and everything changed. From the first paragraph I felt I was holding my breath. That someone could mingle dreams, whorehouses, Paris, roaches, hunger and miserable conditions, syphilis and art, was interesting on its own; but the language and conceits existed on another level entirely, as did Miller's rough and confident disregard for authorial niceties. In time another US writer came along, William Gaddis, whose books changed how I would look at arranging themes, and who resembled Miller in showing what a sentence could contain, and in the sheer brio of the narrative attitude.

After Gaddis, no US writer had come close to providing both that immediate rush of excitement and the encouragement—*incitement* might be more accurate—to innovate until I read

Gilbert Sorrentino's *The Moon in Its Flight* (2004). Obviously Sorrentino wasn't the only one writing something different, but he was the one I came across. Dalkey Archive publisher John O'Brien stated recently that Sorrentino was an "utter master of contemporary fiction who has yet to be discovered and appreciated."[12] With its dismantling of stories, *The Moon in Its Flight* completely overturned my view of what a story could look like when written by someone who put structure above plot and character. As Miller said in *Sexus* (1949), "People have had enough of plot and character. Plot and character don't make life."

Miller, Gaddis, and Sorrentino: They're all no-nonsense talkers when they want to be, at times abrasive, and inventive in ways that appealed to me, and that I needed. *The Moon in Its Flight* came as a relief, and a wonder. The title story has many of its sentences recycled in "Times without Number," another story from the collection, and their interchangeability matches the interchangeability of themes and characters. In "Sample Writing Sample," the narrator says: "This is how literature works, if 'works' is the word." Every story, and all Sorrentino's work, rebuts what we were endlessly taught: Literature contains singular imagery, the perfect word lodged in its perfect spot, rounded characters, believable settings, a confident narrative (if not a confident narrator). This demolition liberates readers, and writers, from stale expectations, and stylistic and aesthetic molds. If you're not going to make words matter in the way we were taught they should, why spend time trying to make the characters loveable? "He wasn't intrinsically contemptible," a narrator says in *The Abyss of Human Illusion*, "yet there was no way, it seemed, that he could avoid being thought of with contempt, at least not by those who got to know him, men and women alike." Sorrentino's men and women, with simple names pinned to them, and dressed in threadbare qualities, come across as what they appear to be—devices. That quality grew more overt in his later work whereas earlier, in a novel like *Mulligan*

Stew (1979), characters are sometimes drawn from other novels (e.g. *The Great Gatsby, Finnegans Wake*). This compares to Raymond Queneau's *We Always Treat Women Too Well*, where the characters' names are lifted from *Ulysses*. Sorrentino liked Oulipian restraints; he is quoted as saying, in conversation with *Publisher's Weekly*, that "form not only determines content, form *invents* content."[13]

Each of Sorrentino's books after 2000 rejuvenated my aesthetic thinking. How can one resist the intellectual and smart-ass charm of *Gold Fools* (2001), a Western told only in interrogatives, that mixes time periods freely as five men (two old and three young) search for gold?

Was Billee flirting with the ineffable realm of the *langue*? Or the equally ineffable, and more expensive realm of the *parole*? Or had he, 'twixt sleep and wake, entered the world of 'competence' and 'performance'? Did Billee know what he was doing, or thinking, or was he the same know-nothing, Jesus-waving sod he'd always been? And yet, had the paradoxes of language somehow chosen him for their own? Their own what?

Now *The Abyss of Human Illusion* (2010) has come out, prefaced with "A Note to the Reader" by his son Christopher, who writes that like most of the late works, it "offers a less apparent and/or more indeterminate structure." And, its "formal ambitions remain unclear (to me)." We are presented with 50 stories or vignettes bearing Roman numerals instead of titles, followed by a section called "Commentaries." The structure resembles the 52 vignettes of *Little Casino* (2002)—a card-game structure—the 53 features of the moon affixed to reviews of art exhibits in *Lunar Follies* (2005), or the 52 sections of *A Strange Commonplace* (2006) where 26 titles are each used twice.

The Abyss of Human Illusion begins: "Mundane things, pitiful in their mundane assertiveness, their sad isolation. Kraft French dressing, glowing weirdly orange through its glass bottle..." The commentary asserts that no one has "suggested a reason for [the dressing's] strange, pumpkin-like color. It is highly popular."

Being "highly popular" wasn't likely for Sorrentino's work, or for him, given his personality. This may be the place to say that when Sorrentino's third novel, *Imaginative Qualities of Actual Things* (1971), came out it, in the words of Joseph Tabbi,

> enjoyed some notoriety as a roman à clef. It made enemies, it caused a stir, and it was then largely forgotten as the living models for the characters, like the author himself, left the scene. It was read by some for its scathing portrayal of local poets and downtown painters, for its faces and names—the ones dismissed by John Cale and Lou Reed as posers, self-abusers, or "just alcoholics."[14]

(Of course, it is more than that, as is shown by the casebook in which Tabbi's article appears.) Sorrentino's popularity—or acknowledged literary presence—according to David Andrews, "peaked in 1980 when he published *Aberration of Starlight*,"[15] which Gerald Howard, in a *Bookforum* piece that came out shortly before Sorrentino's death in May 2006, considers "a book that manages to combine his signature formalism, emotional directness, and clearly autobiographical content with a heart-breaking emotional effect."[16] This book followed *The Orangery* (1978) and *Mulligan Stew* (considered by Eugene Lim to be "the metafiction masterpiece"[17] and by Paul Quinn as "a contender for the title of the most representative work of literature of the postmodern period"[18]). Changes in taste and in the publishing industry meant that despite these three successive achievements the novels of Sorrentino's middle years (the 1980s and 1990s) were largely ignored, though he was kept in print by different houses, notably Dalkey Archive and Coffee House Press. He has his devoted readership (you either get him or you don't, I think), comprised of more, if not many more, than "devoted sons and other deviants," as his son jokes, or the "devoted, few"[19] Deborah Friedell referred to in 2006 when reviewing a reissue of *Aberration of Starlight* (originally published in 1980).

Selling himself to get a readership had never been a concern of Sorrentino's. ("Essentially, the novelist, the serious novelist, should do what he can do and simply forgo the idea of a substantial audience."[20]) But I think how my reading life changed because of him, and how there are other readers who haven't felt that shift, but could yet. He is playful with form—and often has fun at the expense of others, though there's not much fun in *Red the Fiend* (1995), where a 12-year-old boy is abused by his Grandma (while Mother and Grandpa look on, or join in). Even in this relentless novel, Sorrentino instills lists, improbable situations, and much else with humor of different colours. "Red goes out of his way to see if anybody he knows is in the park or the lots, and as he walks beneath the peeling sycamores, he sees a bird fluttering amid the leaves. He stops, picks up a sharp stone, and throws it at the bird. For something to do. To add his little bit to the general cruelty. To be in touch with the spirit of the world." After disposing of the dead bird, Red feels "as if he is, just for a moment, one with the vast entropic rhythms of the earth." A brutal life, one would say, with a grim humor that doesn't do one damn thing to reduce Red's suffering at the hand of his dreadful Grandma.

However—with Sorrentino, there's often a "however"— consider the fact that Grandma appeared in earlier novels, used for this and that purpose, in this and that guise, as have other permutations of the content, so that she and the material are variations on notes and themes we've encountered elsewhere in his books. What, then, of the gloss of reality overlying *Red the Fiend*? Is this a *realistic* novel after all? If it isn't, then where's the abuse? If there's no abuse, then what's the source of the anger we feel, or the despair, or anything that might be engendered by black specks on white paper? What we've spent time reading was a collection of words—well-crafted, pulsing with life—but not necessarily the experience of a young boy and his dismal family. It's fiction, nothing more, and definitely not a bit less: an illusion that has depths we may never see the bottom of.

The small stable of caricatures stemming from Sorrentino's earliest fiction to his last novel include not only permutations of Grandma, but divorced men, soldiers and ex-soldiers, old men who have outlived their spouses and whose children rarely visit, women who committed adultery or have been the victims of it and now live alone, men who like to wear hats, people who play cards, a lot of drinkers, and many kinds of artists (all seen as contemptible). In *The Abyss of Human Illusion* the latter are charlatans, or written out. "The young actress" who married an older writer "grew bored with the marriage, discovering, after a year or so, that writers are, by and large, even more boring than their books..." Steve wants to get his stories accepted by *The New Yorker*, to which his friend says, "I once suggested that he send his stories to a magazine that was, well, not as impressed with itself but he gave me, as it is said, a *look*." Another man has a friend who "is a great success in the small, almost always weaselly world of poetry, its sweaty ambitions, its miniscule rewards, its grim teaching appointments, its pathetic prizes, its insincere enthusiasms." There's no privileging any class or vocation in Sorrentino's world.

Nor do the finer sentiments receive an easier time. If a romantic or sentimental view of writing, or love or anything, pops out for a moment, then it is held up against its opposite. But that doesn't mean that his prose doesn't carry, "as it is said," resonance and emotional freight. In "XXXVII" a marriage just a year old already has problems. "Perhaps," the husband thinks, his wife:

wasn't aware of how she treated him, how she talked to him with equal measures of impatience and patronization, wasn't aware of how she was to him... It never occurred to him that if his wife consciously acted toward him in the manner he thought—he knew—she did, that she might like it, that she might like doing this to him, that she had married him so that he would always be near, waiting patiently to be insulted and demeaned.

When this kind of insight appeared in earlier books they struck me one way, and now they strike me another; which is to say, now that I'm divorced they contain greater power.

I would foolishly explain my idea of writing an Oulipian novella to my (now) ex-wife, who had already chosen, though I didn't know it, not to read any published work of mine (on the grounds that it was "private," though that reasoning is still a mystery to me). She then washed her hands, so to speak, of my vocation, and therefore of a large portion of me. Coming across the passage quoted above I laid down *The Abyss of Human Illusion* and walked away. Not because of an exact parallel, but it felt uncomfortably close. My ex-wife stated emphatically that my Oulipian novel would be an "academic exercise" read by no one. There was a snort before that pronouncement. Being in love, and a bit of a fool, as well as dumbfounded—like Charlie Brown having believed that Lucy wasn't going to pull the football away—I said nothing. To a certain degree I had once shared the imagination of the husband quoted above. Sorrentino's insight into the dynamics of a marriage suddenly illuminated part of my own experience.

The last tale in *Abyss*, "L," is followed by commentaries that provide information for each section (a similar device is found in *Little Casino*). "Some of these commentaries may not be wholly reliable," the narrator says at the end, after we have learned about or are reminded of products, radio programs, and more.

Speaking of "X" he writes: "You might wish to make on the fly leaves of this book some of the things you can dream up, if you wish; the reader is the ruler." In a novel, let alone a life's work, that stresses the beauty of restrictions and the fecundity found in artificiality, we know Sorrentino has always been in charge, no matter what we may prefer out of sentimentality for a more pleasant ending, or from reading literary theory.

A Brooklyn boy who spent time in California ("a reluctant resident"), Sorrentino returned home towards the end of his life. It's fitting, then, to end off speaking about him by quoting my first literary influence—Henry Miller, from Brooklyn—who said about writing: "All that the critics write about a work of art, even at the best, even when most sound, convincing, plausible, even when done with love, which is seldom, is as nothing compared to the actual mechanics, the real genetics of a work of art."[21]

*

Brecht at Night, by Mati Unt (trans. by Eric Dickens)
TWR, 13 December 2010

In the last few years the works of Estonian writer Mati Unt (1944–2005) have been published in translation by Dalkey Archive Press.

The latest, Brecht at Night (1997; Eng. trans. 2009), combines, among other things, criticism of Bertolt Brecht's role as the workers' writer, Estonian history, and postmodernist playfulness. In his introduction Eric Dickens writes: "Shall we continue to call it a 'novel,' or shall we, like W. G. Sebald, insist on avoiding the term?" and that's a question readers will decide for themselves.

At the start of Brecht at Night the German playwright is fleeing to Finland in the spring of 1940 to escape the reach of Nazi Germany. His admiration for Marxism, along with being Jewish, have marked him as an enemy in his homeland. In Finland he waits for the chance to escape elsewhere, hopefully the United States. Mostly Brecht makes love to one or the other of the females who have fled with him, considers his future, worries about Hitler, and wonders dialectically about various matters.

As Brecht ceaselessly analyzes things in abstract terms ("Nothing to be done if the un-dialectical tactics of the interim Soviet government have caused more enlightened minds to move to the right," runs a typical thread of Brecht's thought), Estonia and the other Balkan countries are losing their independence and becoming satellite states of the USSR. Unt's delving into parts of Estonia's wartime history, such as the effects on it of the Molotov-Ribbentrop Pact, and the examination of the actions of several individuals during the Second World War, take in betrayal of country, servitude, and death. These are matters Brecht's brilliant mind can't, and won't, encompass.

Unt's Brecht is a figure based on real events from the playwright's life, but is not a rounded character; Unt's not much interested in the other characters either, and even less in crafting a sweeping linear narrative (and so far as I can tell, never has been). When he discusses being in Finland as the USSR collapsed and relates it to Brecht's nomadic life in the 1940s — "The situation reminded you of the film Casablanca..." —it's not to indulge his ego. Nor is it (as required by novelists nowadays) a tiresome pairing of characters in the present world to a distant ancestor whose secret life they've discovered. Another crummy historical novel isn't what Unt is writing. So, what is *Brecht at Night* about?

It's about something more important than characters and plot lines. It's about something profound that's not handled often today in fiction. It's about the loss of a nation, with everything subordinated to that. This tragic story retrieved from history contains an emotional charge comprising anger, sadness, and bitterness. What couldn't be uttered while Estonia was part of the USSR ("During the Soviet era, from the 1960s... Unt never overstepped the mark," Dickens writes) can now be said openly to enlighten those who are unfamiliar with what transpired in the Baltic in the Second World War. Some passages call to mind the lacerating takes on the mendacity and machinations of tyrants and politicians found in Solzhenitsyn's *The Red Wheel*. Characters, plot, and scenery matter little when a country is disappearing in front of the world's eyes.

The marvel of this novel is Unt's balancing act. *Brecht at Night*, despite Dickens' reservation about what to call it, is a novel that avoids becoming a documentary or polemic; in merging genres (biography, anecdote, personal experience, and historical documents) with irony and self-awareness, the style is postmodernist, yet those emotions referred to earlier keep the tone from being smug or distant. (Unlike Brecht, one grows to realize.) Thanks to its formal constraints, *Brecht at Night* is engaged with life and holds its fury in check. The somewhat disturbed surface of the novel tells us about Brecht's nomadic life, his opinions on Stanislavski (Unt was a director and playwright), and something about the nature of the women in his harem; underneath that flows Finnish life, where "a peace and friendship agreement between that country and the Soviet Union" exists, in troubling fashion, since Finland lost the Winter War to Russia in March 1940; below these layers, like a benthic storm, is what the Soviet Union is accomplishing in Estonia.

The narrative voice that tells us of these things can be tricky occasionally to figure out. Here's a typical passage from a more fictional part of the novel:

On the Friday, Brecht is sitting in the railroad station restaurant with the Finland-Swedish poet Elmer Diktonius.

Diktonius is a proletarian author. At least that's what Brecht has thought since he found out that Diktonius had been the music teacher of the head of the Terijoki government, Otto Ville Kuusinen. What Brecht and Diktonius do not of course know is that Kuusinen's wife is right now wading through the icy River Ussa, in the direction of the labor camp at Vorkuta in deepest Russia. Thirty women prisoners have arrived from Kochmes and some are walking barefoot through the freezing water. Nor are these two men the only ones who don't know. No one knows this. Kuusinen's wife has disappeared without trace. And not even Kuusinen knows where his wife is, and presumably doesn't want to know, as it is better not to have any connection with an enemy of the people. Brecht regards Kuusinen as the true leader of the Finnish proletariat.

A later passage, titled "Where Did They All Vanish To?" summarizes various people's fates:

Riigivanem (i.e., Prime Minister) F. Akel... was arrested by the organs of the People's Commissariat for Internal Affairs on 17th October 1940 and shot in Tallinn on 3rd July 1941. His final resting place is unfortunately unknown. Friedrich Akel was the last of the former state officials of the Estonian republic that was shot before the deportation of those arrested began. Before him, four leading state officials had been shot...

The Estonian consul in Turkey, Ernst Veberman... was arrested by the Cheka on 20th December 1940. On the next day, Stalin's birthday, he ended his life by suicide in the prison in Tallinn.

If you leaf through the criminal cases where the Special Chamber Commission sentenced people to be shot, you can find people who were no longer alive when sentenced.

This passage comes from an account by Vladimir Pool, a former KGB official, published in an Estonian newspaper in 1991 that Unt reproduces. Unless it's a trick of the translation, the similarity of tone in both passages is deliberate. Unt is skating

close to officialese, which on one level is far from Brecht's
theorizing or poetry (quoted often), yet on another not too far
from the distancing from reality Brecht encourages:

> Brecht wanted an actor (and an individual) to see himself
> from the outside. Brecht was a proponent of estrangement
> and alienation.
>
> At any given moment you should be able to ask yourself:
> what is going on? What is happening now?

What is going on is evident, but not to Brecht. His lack of
awareness, in the circumstances, is monstrous. Here, fiction
achieves what analysis alone can't: it brings together subjectivity
and judgment on a subject, and through inventive juxtaposition
shows us not just what history was like, but how it felt to be
dragged through it, and what we need to do to learn from the
experience—to empathize. It is impossible to imagine Brecht
being able to offer any comforting words to Akel, Veberman, or
Kuusinen's wife; such advice as 'seeing yourself from outside'
would not be bracing in their circumstances; it could only be
cruel, or, at the most benign, an impossible luxury.

More so than in the exquisite and humorous *Things in the
Night* (1990; Eng. trans. 2006) and the vampire-driven *Diary of a
Blood Donor* (1990; Eng. trans. 2008), Unt speaks openly about the
damage Soviet rule caused and the blindness ideology causes in
everyone, artists and politicians included. In *Brecht at Night* we
have a fresh example of how fiction can rescue us from forget-
fulness, and from worship of Great Ideas and Great Men.

*

Night Soul and Other Stories, by Joseph McElroy
LR, Spring 2011

Night Soul and Other Stories displays how Joseph McElroy explores what connects people, states of being, and things—"The lake was part of the canoe..." ("Canoe Repair")—and how this approach, present in his novels too, and perhaps the only way to do justice to such entanglements, starts with re-imagining sentences from the ground up.

McElroy, like Xides the architect in "Mister X," the richest story in this collection of 12, is a "risk-taker known for the future, for humane blueprints," and we, the readers, have to get involved and remain involved (going against Robert Glick's disparagement in *American Book Review* of "our quite bizarre expectations that we read every word, that we do not drift in and out of texts"[22])—we must be *attentive,* so as to witness the disappearance of the separation between us and what's going on (not solely the action of the story, but the process), aided in this engagement by the reiteration of the word "you" that, as in McElroy's 1987 novel *Women and Men*, for example, simultaneously is aimed at a character and we, the readers, so that we become part of the narrative, though maybe we resist with: Hey, how close does he want us to get, how close do we want to get?

The stories, some of which go back to the early 1980s, pack an intensity that's intellectual and, when they work best, emotional, though calling them stories does a disservice to their extravagant natures, their rude health, their expansiveness, the gesture they make, indirectly pointing to, acutely aware of, the shrivelled nature of contemporary stories that are tidy, hemmed in, that take up little space (and yet too, too much) and offer little back, so that this collection may be a *rude* gesture toward the writers of spiritually-malnourished offerings, evoking instead, in one case, the genial boulevardier Henry Miller of "A Saturday Afternoon" in the story "The Man With the Bagful of Boomerangs in the Bois de

Boulogne" that contains what might be considered a description of McElroy's efforts, as the man with the boomerangs "aimed each of those bonelike, L-shaped, end-over-end handles along some plane of air as if with his exacting eyes he must pass it under a very low bridge out there before it could swoop upward and slice around and back, a tilted loop whose moving point he kept before him pivoting his body with grim wonder and familiarity."

That "grim wonder and familiarity" illustrates McElroy's seemingly bottomless, delighted astonishment that people do this or that, and *A Smuggler's Bible* (1966), *Lookout Cartridge* (1974), *Actress in the House* (2003), for example, are books sent out on the equivalent of "planes of air" under the "very low bridge" (erected by writers who don't strain for higher altitudes?) and noticed by those who gravitate to him, or to his science-fiction/technology concerns displayed in *Plus* (1977), present here in two speculative stories—"The Campaign Trail," featuring people, "[a]s God was their witness," who resemble Obama and Hilary Clinton, a contemporary Adam and Eve (enjoy its Christian, Hemingway, and Wallace Stevens' allusions), and "The Last Disarmament But One," a science fantasy about a landlocked nation that commits suicide without endangering surrounding countries, leaving behind indestructible "refugee body-souls," as one child puts it—and reminding us how it feels to meet again McElroy's trademark, which, you might say, is the presentation of multiple planes of relationships and existence, where "some wholeness always unfolding" takes in past, present, and future, everyone and everything, frequently rooted in domestic details like an occupation (McElroy's fiction populated by savants who, not idiots, yet stumble and misread like us) or a marriage close to collapse with children at risk, where what one says can be appropriated (see "Annals of Plagiary," calling to mind *The New Yorker*), where it's underscored that, as one character notes, "We say things. People are affected by them," where your experiences merge, if you're in the mood or lucky, with those drawn so well in these stories in a way that can be a mystical experience.

In *Night Soul and Other Stories* we are faced, too, with a subtle mind, highly refined, dealing, at times, with appearances that are almost class-like — "Silk, or the Woman With the Bike" features one bicyclist, prone to or fond of or afflicted with "thinking ahead, to what he did yesterday, the day before, and the day before that, and what he again would do today," a typical McElroy creation, who encounters an abrasive woman whose "bike perhaps suited her, but she was not quite a bicyclist" — and with ethnicity, when a Muslim family is targeted by the government in "No Man's Land," the first story and the collection's weakest; similarly, where memories of a model whaleboat (in "Character") are tied up with too many things, the customary energy in McElroy's writing becomes dissipated, unlike the swirling activity around a family in "The Unknown Kid," featuring a child's question, "'Then why did you bother to have me?'" which is skillfully modulated over the course of the story, always coming back with more in it than it had before, like a wave or energy field, everything changing shape as we read, not least thanks to our involvement as readers, spoken to throughout the book, as we discern shifting meanings.

The collection concludes with the title story, and here McElroy isn't building sentences so much as going for the origin of sounds, with a father looking at his newborn son in the desert night, more accurately listening to his first sounds "in an order more raw and stately — '*uh, ah, eh, ih, aw,*'" the father's palpable desire — "all he wants is to know what the child knows" — completely fruitless, for this man, like so many other characters, "has seen the future and should find tomorrow night that his child has left him with elements no longer of much use and has gone on," the narrative making it clear that Age cannot catch up with Youth, that the vaster experience cannot overtake a child's knowledge, and maybe this is humility on the part of Joseph McElroy as he enters his ninth decade, while we, like the pianist Vic's audience in "Particle of Difference," are "listeners who… absorbed, forget to reach for [our] drinks," while we wonder where his imagination will bring us next.

*

The Truth About Marie, by Jean-Philippe Toussaint (trans. by Matthew B. Smith)
QC, 5 December 2011

In no particular order, here are some things the unnamed narrator tells us about Marie in Jean-Philippe Toussaint's latest work to appear in English. She is happy to wear flip-flops that are "barely attached," and leaves her bathing suit "carelessly on the kitchen floor" of her dead father's house. She's unable to act when faced with a man having a heart event, forgetting her own address while talking to the emergency services. When Marie's passport is needed urgently she roots through about two-dozen pieces of luggage with "that strange mix of panic and goodwill she displays when looking for something." Her usual attire is a long t-shirt with nothing on underneath (though she will be caught wearing less than that), and she often arrives late for appointments. An internationally known artist, she is sensual, sexually available, and eager, but also awkward around the narrator, her former lover. Soon into this charming novella he occupies the uneasy position of a needed friend she appreciates and hates "with a passion." Yet he feels drawn to her afresh, even finding her disorganization a form of "ravishing insouciance, enchanting and radiant, a clear display of Marie's charm at its best," though he immediately adds that it "was delightful as long as one wasn't directly involved."

That's a mistake on the part of the narrator, for a reader of *The*

Truth About Marie can't help but think her selfish, insular, and thoughtless. There's nothing delightful about a woman whose dim-wittedness forces her male friend, the ailing Jean-Christophe, lying on the bedroom floor in her apartment, "pale and sweating profusely, a blank stare in his eyes," to grab the phone from her in an attempt to save his life. Marie is also a mystery, for we don't see much art from this artist, and her own nature is never given directly, but mediated through the narrator, who abruptly leaves another Marie lying in bed in his own apartment to assist his former girlfriend after her call in the middle of the night: "Marie, upset, confused, bewildered, had called me for help, pleading with me to come quickly, without any explanation, come quick, she told me hurriedly, come right now, hurry, it's an emergency, beseeching me, begging me to get to the rue de la Vrillière at once." That she can't get out of what's going on predates this book. In Toussaint's 2009 novel *Running Away*, which also featured Marie and the narrator, she calls him long-distance about her father's death, "not sobbing, her voice seemed calm, if trembling a little bit, out of breath, in a hurry to tell me, in great confusion." The narrator listens intently for some pages, enticed by "the frail and sensuous texture of Marie's voice." She doesn't ask after the narrator, whose life she has interrupted half a world away, she just talks ceaselessly down the line, as incapable then, as she is in *The Truth About Marie*, of thinking outside her own thoughts.

What we have in this attractive novella, then, is a picture of two essentially uninteresting people; but fortunately Toussaint has given the narrator the gift of thinking in delicious prose, describing, in detail: what first responders do; what the narrator believes happened the night of Jean-Christophe's incident; what a scared horse running around an airport does as men struggle to capture him; and the sight and effects of a forest fire. Toussaint keeps well away from the parsimonious dictates of realist fiction, despite the detailed how-ness of certain activities, and appeals to us, through his exquisite breath control, on the level of the long, sinuous sentences that at times transform into grand passages. What's attractive here is the solo performance of the narrator's thoughts, and the easy control Toussaint exhibits.

That control starkly contrasts with the passivity of the narrator who rarely is an initiator. Events and people's emotions (primarily Marie's) wash over him; as best he can, he reflects on them, at times amplifying what he's heard. Toussaint shows the narrator's mind at work while also letting us see the pacing of the book:

> Marie's call—it was a little before two in the morning, this I'm sure of, I looked at the time when the phone rang—had been extremely brief, neither of us able nor really wanting to talk, Marie had simply called for help, and I was speechless, paralyzed by the fear of a late-night call, a feeling confirmed, exacerbated even, by the irrational and violent onrush of embarrassment, annoyance, and guilt I felt immediately upon hearing Marie's voice.

Despite the urgent need to get to her place, the narrator pauses to differentiate between this Marie and the Marie he leaves in bed. On the next page he leaves his apartment at "two thirty in the morning" out into a heavy summer rain, losing his way due to the weather. "I was still running when the Place des Victoires came into sight." He resumes, "on wobbly legs, soaked from head to foot, still moving forward... but no longer running, walking slowly, graceless, as if holding back each step and yet advancing against my will, no longer wanting to go on, imagining the worst." Two pages later: "I was still about a hundred feet from [Marie's] building, and I'd stopped running, I was walking briskly, picking up my pace and slowing it down at the same time, in the same contradictory movement, the same propelling force, the same conflicted stride." A slow, almost regretful advance, which is how *The Truth About Marie* is told; and we are given details by the narrator who seems to have an ability to construct events he never witnessed, and so we question what he's told us.

One such event involves Jean-Christophe's horse, Zahir, aboard a plane as it flies through yet another storm. (The two storms may be seen as emblematic of the emotions running through the characters, or it may be that Toussaint simply likes their possibilities. Beach episodes occur in this book and *Running Away*, as if he's combining the same elements in different ways to show his virtuosity as well as the potential of such scenes.) After giving us the thoughts of Marie and Jean-Christophe, the narrator, who was not on the plane, writes this: "Zahir was aware of nothing but the certainty of being then and there, he had that certainty shared by all animals, silent, tacit, infallible. What lay outside his stall remained unknown to him, the sky, the night, the universe. The power of his imagination stretched no farther than the space in which he stood, his mind was stopped at the walls of his stall and could only return to the confusion of his own hazy consciousness." Obviously, the narrator has an unhampered imagination, since he can present Zahir's feelings as if they were his own. He assumes he knows the horse, like he knows "Marie's every move, I knew how she would have reacted in every circumstance, I knew her instinctively, my knowledge of her was innate, natural, I possessed absolute intelligence regarding the details of her life: I knew the truth about Marie."

That astonishing statement is left untouched, but later the narrator admits his limits:

I could reconstruct [a particular night] in mental images with the precision of dreams, I could cover it in words with a formidable power of evocation, all in vain, I knew I'd never reach what had been the fleeting life of the night itself, but it seemed to me that I could perhaps reach a new truth, one that would take its inspiration from life and then transcend it, without concern for verisimilitude or veracity, its only aim the quintessence of the real, its tender core, pulsing and vibrant, a truth closer to invention, the twin of fabrication, the ideal truth.

On closing this book we can, for a time, remain captured by the fact that its core is that "the truth about Marie" can mean that the truth lies *around* Marie, but does not contain her; and that only art—the transcendence from sheer reality—offers us a higher truth. The narrator is reaching for the all-seeing eye of the subjective artist. But Jean-Philippe Toussaint has reached that level through his use of words, making us see, if only briefly, the improbable as real. Is Marie sensuous and worth the trouble? *Pfui!* The writing is the achievement here, and the delight, and amusement, in watching a deeply talented author wring such descriptions and visions from a love-struck narrator.

*

Kissed By, by Alexandra Chasin
RCF, Summer 2008

Some readers will agree with a blurb on the back of *Kissed By* that labels Alexandra's Chasin's debut work of fiction "experi-mental." It's not as if experimental writers can be easily profiled, separated from the main stream of writers into a straggly line leading to a holding area where authoritarian Contract novelists inspect the baggage of shadowy literary figures who require detention. Gabriel Josipovici stated in an essay that reviewers view experimental writing as "a sub-branch of fiction, rather like teenage romances or science fiction perhaps," and Gilbert Sorrentino regarded the word as a "euphemism for that work which cannot be called 'serious.'" Chasin is an exploratory writer. The 18 pieces in *Kissed By* roughly divide into those which plunge into the cerebral, the composition of the work being the narrative, and those replete with deep, mature emotions. "Toward a Grammar of Guilt" and "Composer and I" are examples of the first category, where we can enjoy Chasin's political engagement and inventiveness; "B. & G. & I" and "Lynette, Your Uniqueness" exhibit bitterness, wit, and a delighted enjoyment found in listening to sounds and converting them into language. This is not simple play with language because one can—the flaw marring "They Come From Mars" (each word four letters long) and "Kant Get Enough" (filled with puns)—but because it's fun to let the imagination go its merry way. This collection is most serious for being at times humorous, allowing for contrasts and juxtapositions of mood. In Chasin's world, her lovelorn or lovesick creations can hear birds say "Cheater. Cheater. Cheater. Cheater… Read. Weepweep. Read. Weepweep," and make one feel a tug of recognition as well as an appreciation of a truly fine ear.

*

The Short Fall, by Marek Waldorf
TWR, January 2014

Canada has not had great political orators for some time, and there is no incentive to quote the words of former prime ministers from the last 30 years, roughly, for their inspirational value. (Generally the same can be said for presidents, premiers, and so on.) Where once they may have uttered phrases that lived on and could be applied, appropriately or not, to certain situations, what is quoted now usually occurs in a journalistic piece or a ridiculing op-ed or television skit. (Rob Ford's statements increasingly occupy a separate, unnamed category.) While there may never have been a golden age of political oratory in Canada, right now things sound only like tin.

It's not the politicians' fault alone. The school system (from kindergarten to post-secondary), focus groups, consultants, hacks, and the demands for soundbites combine to make it difficult for any long utterance, relaxed in its pace, measured in tone and containing phrases freighted with meaning, to be heard and understood, and when, on the rare occasion, such a sentence is said it can appear faintly pompous, put-on, an affectation in this time of terse statements devoid of commitment or information. Political fearfulness at bold statements and the influence of Twitter make the job of current and future speechwriters difficult. How will they be inspired, or given licence, to write anything for an administration that's more than ornate advertising copy?

It may be for this reason that Marek Waldorf (b. 1965), in his amusing, inventive, non-realistic and formally structured novel, *The Short Fall*, has placed events in the 1990s when the final withering of persuasive rhetoric became evident ("'We want dull. But we also want uplift. We have to make placidity look uplifting.'"), and given the narrative over to Chad, a speechwriter for presidential candidate Vance Talbot. Chad has been almost completely paralyzed by an assassin's bullet that went astray, though if required he is able to get down his thoughts through arduous labour via a keyboard. A person whose profession is to speak for a politician and who can't speak is in a potentially sad situation; a character in the same predicament is a way into an occupation and an elite circle. The mind that permits this view is not a particularly welcoming one.

In party politics there is always a centre of activity: not a political centre on a spectrum of ideologies, but the centre each volunteer or staffer imagines himself occupying due to his own position and ego, and aided by the magnetic force of the person being served:

No doubt, there were others who, like me, believed that they, alone with Vance, were responsible for capturing the limited imaginations of the American public. Vance could do that to you. He could make you feel he was your own private sun... He could make you believe that you, alone, were the only person he needed to convince. All of us—me, Rogers, C.G., Dan, the Captain, Ernie & Bert, Lynn—we believed we were each the linchpin in Vance's campaign. We worked together, not as a team, but as Vance's counterparts. Under the great man's auspices, we tolerated the input of the others, secretly plotting their future amputation: all he needed, we believed, was that strong right hand.

Each functionary sees himself—apart from Lynn, a minor speechwriter who uses Oulipian methods in her speechwriting, this is a resolutely male novel—as a favoured courtier. Belief in Talbot is matched by belief in oneself, as we see early on when Chad states: "Vance Talbot became my pseudonym." At one point Talbot remarks to Chad that "'anyone would think that it's you running for office!'" The speechwriter silently agrees. "Without me, there is no Vance"; and, "in a sense, I *was* running for office. Vance was my candidate. I had staked my future on him." Such close identification means that Chad's actual separation, caused by his incapacitation, throws the narrator into intense turmoil. From the first pages we are in the hands of an embittered ex-employee forced out of an illusory space, away from his ventriloquist's dummy and, on a separate plane, no longer within the orbit of the sun that is now President Talbot. (His win may have been helped by the failed attempt on his life.)

There is also the loss of a homoerotic bond that Waldorf plays with. Chad refers to his feelings for Talbot as "a manly crush," and nothing deeper. It will appear to readers to be more profound than that. "Because on paper at least, Vance belonged to me. We coupled there—that solitary place, where I alone occupied his speech and from which he and only he could deliver my words." A further remark elaborates on this: "Next, I pictured Vance and myself in the voluptuous yaw of an eternal surge... eternally coasting on crowd ecstasy..." Chad doesn't wish to consciously acknowledge the full strength of the attachment, perhaps in order not to increase the painfulness of his separation. As he says in another context, "To my dismay, I could find no lie I was incapable of believing."

Anyone who has read the memoirs and diaries or, put baldly, the final blows and betrayals of confidences written by former close advisors of this or that politician will recognize the bitter, paranoid self-puffery present in *The Short Fall*, and admire it for its depiction of naked self-regard and the jilted nature of those who, for one reason or another, find themselves discarded, while at the same time there exists a disdain for the kind of reality those outside a closed circle would experience.

Chad's condition is irreversible, and his waking hours are spent replaying how he, and not Talbot, was shot in the head. What if it wasn't accidental? What if he had been the target all along? His writer's block after a major speech has rendered him practically useless; meanwhile, Talbot's inexplicable slow descent in the polls ("Nobody could define the moment when everything began to fall apart. No one could find a reason") requires drastic action so that the campaign can become rejuvenated. It isn't hard for Chad to imagine political operatives plotting a brutal rescue strategy. As Canada goes through the Senate scandals or the revelations of Edward Snowden on the Communications Security Establishment Canada working with the National Security Agency during the G-8 and G-20 summits, none of what he says seems improbable.

The Short Fall plays on the word "fall" and its derivatives. The main use occurs around the fall of Chad after the bullet hit, but it thematically refers to his fall from position, and a fall from a short-lived idealistic state verging on, but not quite achieving, religious faith. Two passages will serve to illustrate that last statement. When offered the job as speechwriter, Chad asks to meet Talbot and is granted a meeting over lunch. "I remember it well: a sultry day at summer's end, the air like wet bread..." The hotel setting is filled with images of lighting from the sun and lamps. He takes an escalator and "rode it down... To my right, another set of escalators descended into an amber-lit den area..."

The natural world is represented by a waterfall, plants and exotic birds. "Vance, along with three members of his staff, had been seated in a grotto on the far side of the waterfall... *The second those glass doors slid shut behind me, everything changed.* They had effectively sealed off my past. Prior to that moment, you see, nothing matters." He is nervous: "A pale sweat addressed my thighs." This is the language of a man reborn, especially the sentence Waldorf has italicized. In a few lines we are given the union of pagan and Christian imagery, from the sultriness to the sweat (bringing in, once, again, a sexual aspect to the encounter) and the warmth one associates with the underworld, to the breaking of bread in a grotto, the presence of a pool for a baptism, and the sundering of one's past life from, as Chad continues to describe it, "[t]he here. The now."

Orpheus and Dante come together. The quasi-religious imagery continues with Chad's belief that he came up with speeches because he "wrote from a condition of immanent concurrence." This idée fixe persists into the present of the narrative, when almost 20 months have gone by since the shooting sealed Talbot's bid for president. "It mattered to Vance that I remain alive, it was my duty as his savior to allow him to pay me back." With politics and religion so closely intertwined in the United States for some decades now, Waldorf has put his finger on a nerve and pressed hard.

The formal nature of *The Short Fall* comprises a fine balance of elements: the first-person narrative by a very unreliable narrator ("Sometimes I believe myself quite mad. But saying doesn't make it so. Nor thinking either") obsessively going over how he became a sacrifice to his Sun God's ambition; sections featuring equations and geometric shapes (of lines and letters); different fonts; pages that are mostly blank; and the use of movie terminology (scenarios) as used in political campaigns. For instance, "Third Scenario" divides into video on the left-hand side of the page and audio on the right-hand side. (One may recall Malcolm Lowry's "Through the Panama.") Other scenarios explore the "cryptography" of the speeches Lynn writes. These devices are not distracting nor are they exhibitions of talent for its own sake. This use of intermedia—approaches to a narrative drawing from a variety of media other than text—is appropriate to the way Chad sees the world.

Alone in a hospital room "in... let's say, South Dakota," long after a series of operations and procedures, without facts or the hope of corroboration, without visits from or communications with former co-workers, but with access to video images of his last ambulatory minutes, Chad devises explanations for what happened. Each of the 13 scenarios is like a short film, and they often portray a conspiracy of one sort or another, some involving a campaign figure, a "pint-sized Texas billionaire" who calls to mind H. Ross Perot, and Pynchonesque organizations named the Opposition Research Bureau and the Society of Victims (and their offshoots). Readers can trust none of these entirely; they are either implausible or plausible, but the truth is never discovered.

Among other things, such as lessons on how to write a speech, the search for a system that can accurately determine the tendencies of the voting public, and on the personalities and motors that drive a campaign, *The Short Fall* shows how delusional it is to rely excessively on one person when everyone is fallible, and that the same sort of complacency concerning words can, when a person is isolated, lead to madness. Marek Waldorf has written a visually distinct political novel rich with ideas and approaches, and in his hands political belief and excessive faith in the power of words to convey meaning and truth receive an entertaining drubbing.

*

Shantytown, by César Aira (trans. Chris Andrews)
TWR, 18 March 2014

In August 2013 I started a month-long reading jag of Argentinean writer César Aira (b. 1949), by no means able to read all his many novels, but a few that are available in English, published mostly by New Directions, in preparation for his newest book (in English), *Shantytown* (published November 2013). Apart from the introduction to his methods and approaches that reading *Ghosts* (2008), *The Seamstress and the Wind* (2011), *Varamo* (2012) and *The Miracle Cures of Dr. Aira* (2012) provided, there was the joy of encountering a new novelist whose works amuse, baffle, stretch one's imagination, and reaffirm that the form of the novel is untiring of innovation. For this discovery thanks must go to Scott Esposito, co-author of *The End of Oulipo*, who spoke highly of him in that book.

As Esposito says, "...Aira relentlessly combines genres in a very postmodern frenzy of activity, but the books that emerge from this process feel remarkably whole, and they frequently partake in an original lyricism that pays due heed to the *jouissance* of fiction." In *Shantytown* facets of noir fiction are present— a shady part of town, a crooked policeman, women in trouble— but the purpose is neither to recycle overfamiliar tropes nor upend a genre. Aira has greater ambition, and a fine sense of what can be called menace. In *Shantytown* we are, with each page, slowly denied the expected contours of a noir and given something much less formulaic.

On the very first page Maxi, the gym-going innocent (innocent here means weak and untried), offers his strength to help the "local cardboard collectors to transport their loads." This "act performed once, on the spur of the moment, [that] had developed over time into a job," becomes a regular routine. Maxi doesn't view it as "an act of charity or solidarity or Christian duty or pity or anything like that. It was something he did, that was all. It was spontaneous, like a hobby." Maxi doesn't have the ability to know much of his own thoughts (what character does?), and when others refer to him as a "'meathead' or 'brainless hulk'" the narrator agrees that "they weren't too far from the truth." The inability to comprehend what compels him to assist the poor leads us, from the start, into the various levels of uncertainty that make up *Shantytown*.

Prone to falling asleep as soon as daylight fades, Maxi is unreliable, as the narrator makes clear:

Maxi had never gone that far [into the shantytown], but he'd gone far enough to see: in contrast with the dark stretch of road leading up to it, the shantytown was strangely illuminated, almost radiant, crowned with a halo that shone in the fog. It was almost like seeing a vision, in the distance, and this fantastic impression was intensified by his "night blindness" and the sleepiness besetting him already. Seen like that, at night and far away, the shantytown might have seemed a magical place, but he was not entirely naïve; he knew that its inhabitants lived in squalor and desperation. Perhaps it was shame that prompted the scavengers to say goodbye to him before they reached their destination. Perhaps they wanted this handsome, well-dressed young man, whose curious pastime it was to assist them, to believe that they lived in a distant and mysterious place, rather than going into the depressing details.

Apart, then, from being advised not to trust Maxi's conceptions and perceptions, and the shroud that the garbage collectors throw over their lodgings, the narrative expresses doubt through the use of *almost, might,* and *perhaps,* as well as *fog, fantastic* and *magical.* This language is frequent, and the narrative also leans heavily on the words *if* and *must.* Later in the novel the narrator says: "If God intervened in earthly justice, crimes would be punished straight away. And that could only happen if it had been happening all along, in which case human beings would have adjusted their behavior accordingly... But in the world as we know it, God waits." We are not going to gain access to most of what is going on; instead, we are pushed into confusion. Since this is a noir fiction, maybe that's one of its aims, with the possibility everything will be revealed at the end.

In an article[23] for *The Quarterly Conversation,* "The Literary Alchemy of César Aira," Marcelo Ballvé quotes Aira and provides useful commentary:

In fact, Aira has staked out a very cogent and immensely influential (in Latin America) artistic position that basically says "storytelling at its finest avoids explanations, information, interpretation, etc." In a series of 1988 lectures delivered at the University of Buenos Aires, Aira was clear on this point: "The real story, which we have grown unaccustomed to, is chemically free of explanation... The story is always about something unexplainable. The art of narration declines as explanations are added."

Explanation and information, Aira says, are the currencies of our communicational era, our culture of information-saturated media and scientific analysis. We have become so conditioned by this reality that as readers many of us demand "credible" stories, with explanations, linear causality, and perfectly seamless narrative structures.

The novels mentioned at the opening are like *Shantytown* in their questioning of what can be known. In *Ghosts,* set in an apartment building under construction (equivalent to the development of the book itself), we witness a young girl coaxed to her suicide by the spectral figures of men (who she calls "floury clowns"), but though we read about them, not everyone can see them; in the more absurd *The Seamstress and the Wind*, where a wedding dress is swept into the air (almost as ghostly as the figures in *Ghosts*), "the mad force of events" leads into a liaison between a dressmaker and the wind that's fallen in love with her, only to clash with a Monster (though we are never told what happens, as if Aira had gotten bored with that thread); in *Varamo* a lonely civil servant, whose hobby is taxidermy ("His aim had been to produce a fish playing the piano") and who hears voices no one else does, experiences one bad day only to create, using everything in his life and especially what happens in those 24 hours, "a landmark of Latin American avant-garde writing in the first decades of the twentieth century, *The Song of the Virgin Child*"; and in *The Miracle Cures of Dr. Aira* a possible quack (not a stand-in for the writer despite the shared last name) is hunted by a "cursed ambulance, which had been pursuing him in dreams and throughout wakeful nights, in fantasy and reality, always driving with its siren blasting along the uncertain edge of two realms!"

As Ballvé says, "Like the storyteller of prehistory, Aira is concerned not so much with verisimilitude or realism as he is with that bewitching kernel of mystery that is at the heart of a narrative."

Aira's short books, easily fitted into a jacket pocket, spring from many genres, though it would seem that each form, initially useful as a frame for a given project, becomes eclipsed by the time the last page is reached. An aesthetic distance, a bent towards sociological observations, and a prevalent humour that can be dropped without notice keep readers off balance. The shantytown, and what it stands for, is both (though not always simultaneously) a source of humour and a bleak hole that houses misery. In what may be a sideways comment on it (and perhaps Argentina) a female resident of the shantytown passes on received wisdom to Maxi: "'What poor people? Sir, that's an old-fashioned word. In the old days, there were poor people and rich people because there was a world made up of the poor and the rich. Now that world has disappeared, and the poor have been left without a world.'"

Earlier, the narrator had used similar words, but the tone is different: "Anyway, what poor people? The few [Maxi] saw... looked and behaved like any other Argentines. The only thing that identified them as poor was living in those makeshift dwellings... Those dollhouse-like constructions had their charm, precisely because of their fragility and their thrown-together look. To appreciate that charm one only had to be sufficiently frivolous." A reader might conclude that the narrator is uncaring, as when he appraises the appearance of the carts of the poor as "folk art." Such remarks provoke rueful laughter, as well as appreciation for echoing the voice of power that will not speak on behalf of the disadvantaged.

How are we to regard a narrator who seems to speak without either kindness or complete mockery about major and minor characters, and who denies us the expected conclusion of a novel—that is, a resolution that leaves us wiser and satisfied as we close the book? Our conclusion may be that, as there exist mysteries the narrator shows cannot be pierced, then by extension, since *Shantytown* is an object in our so-called real world, we need to consider that the unknown is as prevalent here as within the walls of fiction. Our complacency is rebutted, and this is emblemized in the final section when a terrific rainstorm floods everything, "leaving only the pure scenography of danger, in which, by definition, nothing could happen." Even language dissolves. "'Heddo,' [Vanessa, Maxi's sister] said, and tried again, grimacing, but without any more success, on the contrary: 'Geddgo ... leglo ...' Then, finally, she got it right: 'Hello!'" From habit characters cling to routine and to seemingly solid things. Four friends at a pizzeria "had to rest their feet on the crossbars of the chairs because the tiled floor was under four inches of water." Will this save them from being inundated?

What can save us? For, like the characters in this and other Aira novels, we look for a solid perch during calamities, and we also assume that, in time, and with effort, we will get to the heart of matters. But suppose we are deluding ourselves, and that what we consider as concrete is illusory, at best transitory, and therefore untrustworthy. It's an unsettling thought, and that constitutes the menace I mentioned earlier. We must take César Aira and his work as seriously as we would any other artist, and upon doing so admit there will be repercussions.

Postface

My reading choices don't so much go against the popular taste as pass it by. An anecdote might illustrate the thinking behind this approach better than an argument drawn from theory. *National Geographic* appeared everywhere, in homes and in medical offices, but by its very ubiquity I assumed, in probably a somewhat simple-minded fashion, that people would talk about its content, sparing me the trouble of reading it. (Yes, I do know how that sounds.) But who would tell me about Queneau's *Exercises in Style*? No one, so I read it myself. I chose the reviews in this collection because, for the most part, the books would not be featured in the national newspapers or even in specialized publications when they had every right to be there. On other occasions, it appeared likely that too few reviewers would pay attention to Toussaint or Newman.

The opinions expressed may be agreed with or termed uninteresting or rebarbative, but in any event they are meant to spark discussion as to what the author meant, what he or she achieved, and what transpired within me on first reading. Never perceived as the final word, they invite a long and wide-ranging conversation. Nor were the reviews written with the daft notion of capturing everything that resides in a work of art. As Eric Ormsby wrote, "if the work is truly good, something will always elude our analysis." In a sense, these reviews incorporate my failures, and hopefully a fruitful kind that encourages other critics to be more successful.

*

Small errors that appeared in the original texts have been corrected quietly, minor additions have been made where needed, and if the review had a title in the original publication that has been dropped, except in the piece on Vollmann. All the editors I've worked with have served me well. Any remaining (or freshly introduced) errors of fact, interpretation (really, eisegesis instead of exegesis), and so on remain my responsibility.

Speaking of editors, they deserve to be credited: Olga Stein, who assiduously edited my reviews for *Books in Canada* and who generously, I think, let a newcomer suggest books for her consideration and most often accepted those suggestions; Maurice Mierau for inviting me to contribute reviews and essays on writing (one of which is re-purposed, and somewhat changed, within the Preface) to *The Winnipeg Review* and for his helpful comments, encouragement, and open mind; Eric Lorberer at *Rain Taxi* whose editorial eye benefitted me; Scott Esposito of *The Quarterly Conversation* whose wide reading and impressive output I deeply respect; and the various talented hands who have served at *American Book Review* and *The Review of Contemporary Fiction* over the years.

Publishers deserve thanks as well, for if they hadn't sent books out, especially in the early years when I didn't have many credits to my name, there would be far fewer reviews. Author responses to this or that review have been few, but on the whole pleasant, barring a couple of exceptions. Each reaction taught me something, so they deserve thanks also. Finally, there are the occasional readers who took the time to read this or that review. It has initiated discussions that mean a great deal, and my thanks go to them as well.

Endnotes

Preface

1   Starnino, Carmine. *Lazy Bastardism: Essays & Reviews on Contemporary Poetry* (Kentville, Nova Scotia: Gaspereau Press, 2012), p. 246.

2   Woods, Stuart. "Writers' Trust shortlist trumpets unsung Canadian talent," [online], *Quillblog*, 2015, Available from: www.quillandquire.com/book-news/2011/09/28/writers-trust-shortlist-trumpets-unsung-canadian-talent/ (Accessed 12 December 2015).

3   Josipovici, Gabriel. "Conclusion: From the Other Side of the Fence, or True Confessions of an Experimentalist," *The Mirror of Criticism: Selected Reviews 1977-1982* (Sussex: The Harvester Press, 1983), p. 173.

4   Gass, William. "Finding a Form," *Finding a Form* (Champaign, Illinois: Dalkey Archive Press, 2009), p. 45.

5   White, Curtis. *Monstrous Possibility: An Invitation to Literary Politics* (Normal, Illinois: Dalkey Archive Press, 1998), p. 68.

6   Motte, Warren. "Margins and Mirrors," *The Review of Contemporary Fiction*, Fall 2013, Vol. XXXIII, No. 3, p. 110.

Part I: Panorama

1   Green, Daniel. "John Domini's transformations," [online], *Open Letters Monthly*, 2014, Available from: www.openletorsmonthly.com/john-dominis-transformations/ (Accessed 11 December 2015).

2   Anonymous. "The Sea-God's Herb: Essays and Criticism, 1975-2014," [online], *Publishers Weekly*, 2014, Available from: www.publishersweekly.com/978-1-938103-78-0 (Accessed 11 December 2015).

3   Sorrentino, Gilbert. *Imaginative Qualities of Actual Things* (Normal, Illinois: Dalkey Archive Press, 1991), p. 61.

4   Bell, Madison Smartt. "William T. Vollmann," *New York*

Times, 6 February 1994, Available from: www.nytimes .com/1994/02/06/magazine/william-t-vollmann.html (Accessed 5 December 2015).

5   In *Riding Toward Everywhere* (New York: Ecco, 2008) Vollmann meets many hobos, among them Cinders, christened the Great Grand Duchess of the Hobos by Frog, the King of the Hobos. Here, as elsewhere, the author is reminiscent of Cendrars, who in *The Astonished Man* (1945) wrote about the internal politics and culture of Gypsies. He had earned their trust, just as Vollmann does from the hobos, gang members and prostitutes he meets.

6   Maslin, Janet. "The Poor Are Different From You and Me. Or Are They?" *New York Times*, 22 February 2007, Available from: query.nytimes.com/gst/fullpage.html?res=9B01EFDE 133EF931A15751C0A9619C8B63 (Accessed 5 December 2015).

7   Gibbons, James. "Time Improvement: William T. Vollmann's Real World," *Bookforum*. Jun./July/August/September 2005, Available from: www.bookforum.com/archive/sum_05/ gibbons.html (Accessed 5 December 2015).

8   Wood, Michael. "Parables of a Violent World," *New York Review of Books*, 15 December 2005, pp. 64–7.

9   Seaman, Donna. "Boxcars, Shostakovich, and the Poor," *Bookforum*, Feb./Mar. 2007, p. 52. Hereafter referred to as Seaman.

10   Quinn, Paul. "With dirty hands," *Times Literary Supplement*, 12 Mar. 2004, pp. 3–4. Hereafter referred to as Quinn.

11   Sturrock, Matt. "Among the World's Downtrodden," *Books in Canada – Canadian Review of Books*. Vol. 36, No. 5 (Summer 2007), p. 13. Hereafter referred to as Sturrock.

12   Vollmann, William. *Rising Up and Rising Down: Some Thoughts on Violence, Freedom and Urgent Means*, New York: Ecco, 2004 [abridged version], p. 45. Hereafter referred to as *RURD*.

13   Wyatt, Edward. "Series of War Stories Wins Book Award," *New York Times*, 17 November 2005, Available from: www. nytimes.com/2005/11/17/books/17books.html (Accessed 12 December 2015).

14   Fort, Charles. *Wild Talents*, New York: Claude Kendall, 1932, p. 32.

15   "A series of small strokes had wrecked my balance," Vollmann writes in *Riding Toward Everywhere*, as he makes his slow way over a breakwater, "anxious not to crack my pelvis again." In addition, "aching ears" are a reminder of his ticket-free time on trains. He has slowed down, but most healthier, fitter writers don't risk trying to board moving trains after avoiding railway security.

16   Vollmann, William. "A Branch of Flowers," *American Book Review*, Nov./Dec. 2006, pp. 4–5.

17   *RURD*, p. 34.

18   Kirn, Walter. "Show Me the Moneyless," *New York Times*, 18 March 2007, Available from: www.nytimes.com/2007/03/18/ books/review/Kirn.t.html?_r=0 (Accessed 5 December 2015).

19   Solzhenitsyn, Aleksandr. "Nobel Lecture," *The Solzhenitsyn Reader: New and Essential Writings 1947–2005*. Eds. Edward E. Ericson, Jr. and Daniel F. Mahoney. Wilmington, DE: ISI, 2006, p. 525. Hereafter referred to as Solzhenitsyn.

20   Sturrock, p. 13.

21   Kristof, Nicholas. "Wretched of the Earth," *New York Review of Books*, 31 May 2007, Available from: www.nybooks.com/ articles/archives/2007/may/31/wretched-of-the-earth/ (Accessed 5 December 2015).

22   Munger, Dave. Untitled review, *The Quarterly Conversation*, Issue 7, Spring 2007. Available from: quarterlyconver sation.com/poor-people-by-william-t-vollmann-review (Accessed 5 December 2015). Hereafter referred to as Munger.

23   Quinn, p. 4.

24 Munger.

25 Krissdóttir, Morine. *Descents of Memory: The Life of John Cowper Powys*, New York: Overlook Duckworth, 2007, p. 345.

26 Seaman, p. 52.

27 Sturrock, p. 13.

28 Solzhenitsyn, p. 526.

29 Quinn, p. 4.

30 Solzhenitsyn, p. 518.

31 Solzhenitsyn, p. 519.

32 Solzhenitsyn, p. 514.

33 Tolstaya, Tatyana. *Pushkin's Children: Writing on Russia and Russians*, New York: Mariner Books, 2003, p. 64.

Part II: Selected Reviews
Canadian Tales

1 White, Curtis. "Managing despair," [online], *Big Other*, 8 March 2012, Available from: bigother.com/2012/03/08/27085/ (Accessed 9 December 2015).

2 Rosenblum, Rebecca, "There is life among the cubicle dwellers," [online], 49th shelf, 29 June 2011, Available from: 49thshelf.com/Blog/%28keyword%29/rebecca%20rosenblum (Accessed 12 December 2015).

3 Dalkey Archive, Available from: www.dalkeyarchive.com/a-conversation-with-s-d-chrostowska-author-of-permission/ (Accessed 5 December 2015).

4 3:AM Magazine. "i wasn't writing a novel," [online], *3:AM Magazine*, 16 December 2013, Available from: www.3am magazine.com/3am/i-wasnt-writing-a-novel/ (Accessed 5 December 2015).

5 World Wide Words. "Green-ink letter," [online], 5 April 2003, Available from: www.worldwidewords.org/qa/qa-gre5.htm (Accessed 5 December 2015).

6 Beattie, Steven. "S.D. Chrostowska's Permission: notes toward a Canadian nouveau roman," *That Shakespearean rag:*

notes from a literary lad, 13 September 2013, Available at: www.stevenwbeattie.com/?p=872 (Accessed 5 December 2015).

Realism and Suffering

7   Gordimer, Nadine. "The main course," [online], *Threepenny Review,* 2014, Available from: www.threepennyreview.com/ samples/gordimer_sp03.html (Accessed 12 December 2015).

8   Musil, Robert. "Helpless Europe," *Precision and Soul: Essays and Addresses.* Trans. Burton Pike and David S. Luft. Chicago: The University of Chicago Press, 1990, pp. 116–117.

9   Wiesel, Elie. "The lives of three Trottas," [online], *New York Times,* 3 November 1974, Available from: www.nytimes .com/books/99/10/31/specials/roth-radetzky.html (Accessed 12 December 2015).

10   Maistrello, Mary. "Ornela Vorpsi: me, Albania and the 'whoring of the human race,'" *CafeBabel,* [online], 18 January 2008, Available from: www.cafebabel.co.uk/culture/article/ ornela-vorpsi-me-albania-and-the-whoring-of-the-human-race.html (Accessed 9 December 2015).

11   Miller, Henry. *Tropic of Capricorn,* New York: Grove Press, 1961, p. 298.

Outlier, Innovators, and Explorers

12   Kellogg, Carolyn. "John O'Brien of Dalkey Archive Press, Part 1," [online], *Los Angles Times,* 16 July 2009, Available from: latimesblogs.latimes.com/jacketcopy/2009/07/john-obrien-of-the-dalkey-archive-part-1.html (Accessed 12 December 2015).

13   Anonymous. "Gilbert Sorrentino," [online], *Poetry Foundation,* Available from: www.poetryfoundation.org /bio/gilbert-sorrentino (Accessed 12 December 2015).

14   Tabbi, Joseph. "Matter into Imagination: The Cognitive Realism of Gilbert Sorrentino's Imaginative Qualities of

Actual Things." *The Review of Contemporary Fiction*, Spring 2003, Vol. XXIII, No. 1, p. 90.

15 Andrews, David. "Gilbert Sorrentino," *The Review of Contemporary Fiction*, Vol. XXI, No. 3, p. 18.

16 Howard, Gerald. "A view from the ridge," [online], *Bookforum*, Feb./Mar. 2006, Available from: www.book forum.com/archive/feb_06/howard.html (Accessed 12 December 2015).

17 Lim, Eugene. "Remembering Gilbert Sorrentino," [online], *The Brooklyn Rail*, July/August 2006, Available from: www.brooklynrail.org/2006-07/lastwords/remembering-gilbert-sorrentino (Accessed 5 December 2015).

18 Quinn, Paul. "The foghorns and the vacant lots," *Times Literary Supplement*, June 17, 2005, p. 19.

19 Friedell, Deborah. *Times Literary Supplement*, 16 December 2006, p. 23.

20 Laurence, Alexander. "Gilbert Sorrentino interview," [online], *The Write Stuff*, 1994, Available from: www.altx .com/int2/gilber.sorrentino.html (Accessed 12 December 2015).

21 Miller, Henry. "Reflections on Writing," *Henry Miller on Writing*, New York: New Directions, 1964, p. 112.

22 Glick, Robert. "Dead Metaphor," *American Book Review*, November/December 2010, vol. 32, no 1, p. 22.

23 Ballvé, Marcelo. "The literary alchemy of César Aira," [online], *The Quarterly Conversation*, 2008, Available from: quarterlyconversation.com/cesar-aira-how-i-became-a-nun (Accessed 5 December 2015).

Contemporary culture has eliminated both the concept of the public and the figure of the intellectual. Former public spaces – both physical and cultural – are now either derelict or colonized by advertising. A cretinous anti-intellectualism presides, cheerled by expensively educated hacks in the pay of multinational corporations who reassure their bored readers that there is no need to rouse themselves from their interpassive stupor. The informal censorship internalized and propagated by the cultural workers of late capitalism generates a banal conformity that the propaganda chiefs of Stalinism could only ever have dreamt of imposing. Zer0 Books knows that another kind of discourse – intellectual without being academic, popular without being populist – is not only possible: it is already flourishing, in the regions beyond the striplit malls of so-called mass media and the neurotically bureaucratic halls of the academy. Zer0 is committed to the idea of publishing as a making public of the intellectual. It is convinced that in the unthinking, blandly consensual culture in which we live, critical and engaged theoretical reflection is more important than ever before.